scm centrebooks · six christi

already published
Martin Luther King / *Kenneth Slack*
Simone Weil / *David Anderson*
Karl Barth / *John Bowden*

in preparation
Sun Yat Sen / *C. R. Hensman*
Teilhard de Chardin / *Vernon Sproxton*
George Bell / *Ivan Yates*

John Bowden

Karl Barth

SCM PRESS LTD

334 00074 2

First published 1971
by SCM Press Ltd
56 Bloomsbury Street London

© *SCM Press Ltd 1971*

Printed in Great Britain by
Billing & Sons Limited
Guildford and London

Contents

Preface

Karl Barth, his life and work, are a good deal to write about in one hundred and twenty-eight pages. Wholesale omissions are inevitable. So I had better start by explaining what I have tried to do and what I have not even begun to attempt.

This book sets out to give a general impression of the sort of person Barth was. I never met him, and there is no full-scale biography of him in any language, so a certain amount of personal reaction to his own written work has been a necessary part of my reconstruction. Fortunately, Barth published a small amount of autobiographical detail and personal correspondence, and there are passing references in a number of his more formal works, so there is some basic material to go on.

By the end of the book it should be evident what I feel about Barth the man, and this may persuade readers to investigate him further for themselves. What will not be found here is anything like an adequate account of his thought. As Barth was above all a thinker, what he thought about has had to be brought into the story in many places. My description will, however, have to be supplemented by the more detailed studies of others – or, better still, by studying Barth himself – if justice is to be done.

I first heard the name Karl Barth at Oxford, and shortly afterwards bought a copy of his *Epistle to the Romans* which I at first put aside, half unread. It is thanks to two Anglican country parsons, T. H. L. Parker and Martin

Cordes, and their profound love for Barth, that I went on reading further. They will disapprove of this book, but I hope that they will forgive me for it. The notes show the many writers to whom I am indebted.

Highgate
November 1970

1 Profile

He would rise regularly before seven and spend about half an hour in reflection. Then he would listen for a while to the music of his beloved Mozart from the library of gramophone records with which his friends kept him well supplied. He would read the newspaper. And then he would work, reading and writing, until early afternoon, even ignoring lunch if he was too preoccupied. At 3.45 p.m., four days a week, he would leave home for his lecture at the university; when that was over he would return to work again, often until well past midnight. More Mozart and detective stories at the end of the day seem to have been his only relaxation. A pipe was his constant companion, but his tastes were simple: a good bottle of wine or the occasional glass of beer, or something out of the ordinary to eat to mark special celebrations, were the only departures from an almost ascetic rigour.[1]

For a celebrated man he travelled remarkably little, and breaks in the routine were few: seminars with the students at home or, later, in the restaurant across the street, visitors, infrequent sermons or lectures – these were about the only interruptions to a pattern kept up with increasing devotion from shortly after the Second World War. Invitations to speak, to write articles or to assess books were discouraged and almost always refused; letters went unanswered. 'I have not sworn to devote myself relentlessly to this work,' he wrote, 'for I know that there is no path from which a man must not allow himself to be summoned if a higher necessity presents itself. My only request is for patience that for the moment I think it right to keep for the most part as firmly as possible to this task unless and until I receive a most urgent summons to the contrary.'[2] That was on his sixty-second birthday, 10 May 1948; his resolve remained firm, the summons elsewhere never came, and only failing strength and recurrent illness in old age succeeded in bringing the work to a standstill twenty years later, not long before his death.

It was never finished, despite all this labour. When he had to reconcile himself to the fact that his plan would not be carried through, he compared what had already been done to Strasbourg Cathedral, to Mozart's Requiem, to Schubert's Eighth Symphony, all unfinished.[3] Ambitious comparisons these may be, but what was finished is impressive by any standards. Thirteen formidable volumes, white in the original German edition and black with a brick-red, plainly printed jacket in the dour Scots-sponsored translation, are immediately recognizable on any library shelves. The smallest volume, the last 'fragment', is a book of over two hundred pages; the other volumes are anything between four hundred and nine hundred pages long; the work as a whole extends over more than eight thousand pages, containing almost six million words.

Those six million words alone would make Karl Barth, their author, a more than prolific writer. But they are only half his output. In his younger days he wrote many other books, pamphlets and articles: a list of publications compiled for his seventieth birthday in 1956 contained no fewer than four hundred and six items.[4] Some are little over a page long, but here too there are books of five or six hundred pages, the results of research that would have taken lesser men half a lifetime for each volume.

10

So the rigorous discipline of the last years was no new thing. The greater physical resources of youth and middle age allowed more deviation from the routine, but the man who added so much to the bibliographies of the world must have spent the greater part of his life with a book or a pen in his hand. And the question arises, what sort of material for a biographical sketch is the monotonous discipline that made the production of so many words possible? Furthermore, of what concern to anyone but the specialist can any writer be who takes so long to say what he has to say? What kind of a story is it that comes out of the solitude of a study?

First of all, we have to see precisely what Karl Barth was reading and writing about, and what he was concerned to do. Here his reputation is perhaps the most direct guide.

Karl Barth was a theologian. Indeed, he was *the* theologian of the first half of the twentieth century. All theologians, at least, have heard his name, even if they have never read a sentence from his works, and every theologian probably has some imaginary picture of him or label for him. Respect for him was not, however, confined to the professionals. Church leaders strove to outdo each other in their praise and made their comparisons with the greatest figures of the Christian tradition. Protestants affirmed that it was necessary to go back to Calvin or Luther to find a thinker of the same stamp. No less a person than Pope Pius XII remarked that Barth was the greatest theologian since Thomas Aquinas. Others have gone still further back, to the classical, formative period of Christian doctrine, and linked his name with those of Athanasius and Augustine, arguably the two supreme writers of Greek and Latin theology. Barth has been accepted among the patriarchs.

At the same time, his early writings put him among the prophets. Without excess of modesty, Barth more than once included his own name in a sequence going back through representatives of the darker, more questioning side of Christianity, with Kierkegaard and Dostoievsky, St Paul and the prophet Jeremiah. Others have not quarrelled with his verdict; indeed, they have said that in the future it is as a prophet rather than a church father that Barth will be remembered.

So Barth was a great theologian. But when that has been said, how much the wiser are those outside the circles of theologians and churchmen? Where does Barth fit into the wider world? What do theologians actually do all day?

Anyone looking at theology in its most flourishing modern home, the university, might come to the conclusion that the theologian's work can consist of almost anything. Courses in modern theology include a wide variety of subjects which have a bearing on religious traditions and their history. Theology, or religious studies, which is being increasingly preferred as a title, can include the learning of ancient languages and the study of ancient texts, whether Greek, Hebrew, Latin, Aramaic, Syriac or Accadian; it can comprise not only Christian doctrine, but philosophy of religion, ethical thought, social history and psychology. Nor are religious studies confined to the Christian tradition; the field can be extended to include Buddhism, Islam, Hinduism, Judaism, the relationship of all these religions to one another and the phenomenon of religion itself against a variety of different cultural backgrounds. Quite enough to keep a man occupied in reading all his days!

Yet all this is not theology as Barth understood it. In his more generous moments he acknowledged the importance of all these facets of religious studies, but for him they were never more than a beginning, and often a false start at that. The growing trend towards names like 'religious studies', 'philosophy of religion', 'phenomenology of religion', would seem, in his eyes, to give the game away. For Barth made a quite fundamental distinction between 'religion' and 'theology', and the two were not to be confused. As we shall see, he regarded 'religion' as something entirely human. It was man's search for God, a search often so fruitless or perverted that it ended in a completely false god. Theology, on the other hand, was, as its name signifies, 'God-talk': not talk *about* God, for God is not an object that can form the content of our discourse, but the human response to the word of God that has already been spoken to man before theology begins. How and if this can be so is a question for later; for the moment it is enough to see that this is what Barth always believed. It is this that marked him out from all his contemporaries and led to the honour in which his name has been held. Those long hours and years in the study were spent struggling with, expounding, developing a new insight into the nature of God which had come to him with explosive force in his early manhood.

All religious practice has a theology, in the sense of an understanding of the nature of God. It may be good or bad, implicit or explicit, but it is there. If it has not been properly thought out, if it is ignored at the expense of liturgy or emotion, if it is inadequately related to its subject, God, if it is too overloaded with purely human cultural or political interests, it is bad theology. Good theologies are rare, and they are fragile. But they always have to be looked for. The individual or the church always has to ask, or be asked, 'Is your thought, your worship, your practice, really directed towards *God*, and not something of your own and for you?' For if it is not, then by talking about God at all the individual or the church is guilty of the worst of all failings, of self-deceit, of claiming an undeserved status. Barth's contribution has been constantly to stress that God

13

is – God. He is beyond all man's contriving, imagining and understanding. He cannot be trivialized.

In a course of theology at a university it is possible to acquire a great deal of knowledge without ever coming up against the thought of the glory and majesty of God and the response demanded by him, the personal claims made by the recognition of the nature of God. Whatever his critics may say of him, Barth's work can never be faulted here. From the beginning, he was constantly aware of the demands of the subject. During the first year of his first university teaching appointment, in the academic atmosphere of Göttingen, Barth wrote to a friend:

> To make you acquainted with my spiritual condition I will report to you what Barthold von Regensburg (AD 1272) once said: 'A man who looks directly into the sun, into the burning radiance, will so injure his eyes that he will see it no more. It is like this also with faith; whoever looks too directly into the holy Christian faith will be astonished and deeply disturbed with his thoughts.'

He went on:

> Often it seems to me problematic to what extent it is both good and possible to spend the thirty-four years that still separate me from my retirement at that task 'being deeply disturbed with thoughts'. To be a proper professor of theology one must be a sturdy, tough, insensitive lump who notices absolutely nothing . . . will I perhaps in time myself become such a blockhead? Or explode? If you can see any third possibility, tell me of it for my comfort.[5]

In the years exceeding his modest estimate, Barth neither became a blockhead nor exploded. He may not altogether have avoided damage to his eyesight – in particular, constant gazing into heaven may have dulled his perception of what was happening around him on earth – but he kept looking, and the light from which he could never for long turn his eyes was refracted through his personality and by his studies of the great thinkers of Christianity and all its major doctrinal tenets, which were consumed by his voracious appetite and re-presented in a new and markedly individualistic form.

Thus far, Barth may still seem the highly intellectual specialist, and hardly the writer for the common man. But that is far from the truth. There seems to be in his books a dimension that communicates on more than a purely intellectual level, remarkably like that achieved by the creative artist. Clergy tired and depressed from unrewarding work in their parish have come home (and in England, too) to find new strength in reading Barth; in his lifetime, the sustenance that Barth provided was even greater. One testimony is to be found in the experience of those who translated Barth's first works into English. Sir Edwyn Hoskyns, the famous Cambridge New Testament scholar, was helped through a severe personal crisis by his task of translating Barth's epoch-making commentary, *The Epistle to the Romans*; Douglas Horton, who translated a lesser-known collection of early addresses, *The Word of God and the Word of Man*, recalled in particularly vivid terms his first meeting with Barth's writing. One day he came across the German original of the book on the 'New Books' shelf in a theological library near the parish where he was serving as minister. At first he glanced idly through it, then began reading some of the more arresting paragraphs, and presently 'succumbed so completely to the spell of its passionate intensity and penetrating faith' that he lost track of time until he came to himself again two or three hours later.[6]

The most impressive testimony of all, however, from the period immediately before the Second World War, is given by an Englishman, Dr John Marsh:

There is one story about Barth that I shall never forget. I was in Germany in the early days of 1938 on the very day when the second volume of his great *Church Dogmatics* was delivered in the post of the German pastor with whom I was staying. It was as if a year's supply of food had come to some beleaguered city that would otherwise have starved to death. I shall never forget the joy and delight of that morning post; and I have never since been able to give much credence to the critics who, from a safe and comfortable Anglo-American study armchair, tell the world that Barth's theology is theoretical and remote. Theoretical, in one sense, of course it must be, if it be theology at all; but remote, no! – not after I had seen how much his writing was a veritable munition of war in the death struggle of the church, which was given victory very largely through the writings of Karl Barth.[7]

This comment is a reminder that Barth's work, theology though it may be and despite his determination to keep it so, has not been confined to a theological context. His thinking caused a revolution in the world of theologians; it also left its mark on the political history of Germany between the wars. For Karl Barth was the leading figure behind the stand taken by the German Confessing Church, virtually the only group of Christians to make a determined and outspoken protest against the policies of the Hitler regime. At that time Barth's word was one for which every Christian waited, and he remained a political force until the end of the war and even after it, with his forthright views about the attitudes to be adopted towards conquered Germany and expanding Communism in the post-war period. When, in April 1963, he joined a group including Winston Churchill, Albert Schweitzer, Igor Stravinsky, Niels Bohr and Bertrand Russell as recipient of the Sonning Prize, awarded for outstanding contributions to European culture, it was clear that here was more than a cloistered academic.

A great theologian, a man whose thoughts communicated themselves to Christians well outside strictly academic circles and on a more profound level, a political inspiration to Western Europe – yet even this is only part of the story. For at this point the problem and paradox of Barth begins. Among the many laudatory obituaries published in English

16

newspapers at the time of Barth's death was one which went beyond the conventional and the obvious and introduced a note of perplexity. Philip Toynbee, writing in *The Observer*, acknowledged Barth's greatness and his contributions to Christian thought. But he could not stop there. 'To someone like myself, who has no claims whatever to theological scholarship or expertise but who has spent many years reading and thinking about religion,' he added, 'Barth has always seemed something of a mystery, and, whenever the mystery appears to lighten for a moment, something of an ogre.'[8] Toynbee picks out two things that puzzle and repel him. First, although many modern theologians confess to having been greatly influenced by Barth, their views on the whole seem to be far closer to what Barth made it his lifelong duty to oppose than to what he strove to uphold. This is strange. Secondly, because Barth has so stressed that God is above man and above man's thinking, because his thoughts and words are not human thoughts and words, because (as we saw) true theology is to be distinguished from human religious aspiration, and from history, profane philosophy, anthropology, the arts, even ordinary human love, all these are devalued and can even be seen as dangerously blasphemous undertakings.

This danger had been seen by others when Barth's first writings appeared. Adolf von Harnack, the great liberal German church historian, asked in the 1920s: 'If God is not at all what he is said to be in the light of the development of culture and cultural knowledge and morality, how can we protect this culture and ultimately ourselves from atheism?'[9] Barth dismissed the question as irrelevant, but it was not. When Dietrich Bonhoeffer wrote from his prison cell about the absence of God in the modern world, about the 'God-shaped gap' in the make-up of modern man, about 'religionless Christianity', he did so under the direct influence of Karl Barth. When Harvey Cox, the American theologian and sociologist, took Bonhoeffer's thought further and talked about the blessings of life in *The Secular City*, he was only taking the approach one step further in a negative direction. Finally, when a disillusioned pupil of Barth's, Paul van Buren, who reinterpreted Christianity completely in this-worldly rather than other-worldly terms in *The Secular Meaning of the Gospel*, took yet another step and contributed towards the appearance of the 'God is dead' slogan in newspapers and magazines in the late 1960s, Barth's thought was again very much in the background. It proved all too easy, for those who could not see the reality of the God to whom Barth's whole approach was a response in faith, to translate his positive but essentially irrational belief into negative and essentially rational atheism.

The point could be taken further in the context of the church; it could be shown how Barth's work has also obscured the problem of modern interpretation of the Bible, failed to provide adequate help for the growing ecumenical movement and hindered the growth of understanding between Christianity and other religions. An assessment of Barth's significance must, however, be postponed for the end of the book. We have seen something of the way in which he is regarded by others; now it is time to take a more direct look at the man himself.

A fascinating sequence of portraits of Barth was assembled to illustrate a collection of autobiographical articles published in celebration of his eightieth birthday.[10] Taken at intervals throughout his life, they give a good impression of the man and his temperament; acquaintances used to comment on the unusual mobility of his features, so that his varied expressions could be read very clearly.

18

First comes Barth the student in his twenties, stiff white collar apparently all of four inches tall towering above a tightly tied black tie and dark suit; pince-nez with a cord reaching back over the ear, pencil moustache and well-brushed black hair; high forehead and cheekbones and an angular nose; head held well up and eyes staring firmly forward, the whole effect rather like an officer released from the parade ground. He never looks quite so neat again.

Fifteen years later, at thirty-eight, Barth the professor looks older than his years. The moustache has grown to more comfortable dimensions and the collar is soft and loosely fitting. The tie has begun to creep down the neck and has a less than immaculate knot; the suit is slightly crumpled and the waistcoat serrated. The left hand is firmly clutching a pipe and the angle of the head and the look in the eyes suggest relaxation, informality, invitation to conversation and friendship. It is an extremely attractive picture; here is the university professor, but it might also be the country parson in his study.

This informality and ease persists throughout the portraits of the older Barth. The moustache disappears, bringing into prominence the lines running down from the sides of the nose to the corners of the mouth, but the face never takes on a melancholy aspect; it is almost as if the extremities of the mouth are slightly puckered up in the beginnings of a smile. And then there are the eyes. One wishes it were possible to see them more clearly beneath the prominent eyebrows and the horn-rimmed spectacles which, as so often happened in lectures, seem to want to slip down the nose. When they can be seen, they are full of expression. They are taking in the world on their terms and summing it up in a judicious and penetrating way. There can be no question of the camera dictating the expression. He is, without question, a nice man.

Those who have met Barth for any length of time confirm the impression given by the photographs. Personal conversations with him were unforgettable. The young Dietrich Bonhoeffer, meeting Barth for the first time in 1931, wrote to a friend that it was 'important and surprising in the best way to see how Barth stands over and beyond his books'.[11] The twinkle in the eye, the readiness to listen, the concentrated attention, all made an indelible mark on those who penetrated the defences and achieved a talk face to face. This sense of delight and enjoyment coupled with complete absorbtion in the matter in hand are not only limited to personal conversation; they are a major characteristic of his written work. So those who can no longer meet Barth but have to come to know him through his books can still find abundant evidence of his personal qualities.

Barth's sense of humour has become almost proverbial. It would be wrong to say that with him there is never a dull moment – there are a good many of them in various areas of his writing – but it is a rare book that does not have one shaft of his penetrating wit. 'Wit' is perhaps the best word from which to enlarge on this side of Barth's character, for it is a varied and complex part of his make-up. From the beginning, Barth was a master at words, at throwing up verbal pictures and images, at pointing phrases. Some say that this is a gift of the natives of Basel, Barth's home; if so, few citizens can have been endowed with it to such a degree.

Barth's wit is a mixed blessing. At worst it can be a vicious weapon of destruction, so that one American theologian called him a 'verbal sadist'. Even so, provided that one agrees with Barth, his irony and ridicule to the point of maliciousness can be extraordinarily entertaining. If Barth could be right all the time and his opponents as foolish and incompetent as he makes out, then everything would be splendid. Unfortunately, he is not omniscient, and if one has more than a little sympathy with the other side, the same wit can appear all too heavy-handed, and, where he misses a point completely (as he sometimes does), can be infuriating in the extreme. Those who want to confirm this impression at first hand should first read a little of the writing of Barth's contemporary Rudolf Bultmann and then turn to Barth's short study, 'Rudolf Bultmann, An Attempt to Understand Him' (the title itself is meant to be humorous, as 'understanding' is a key concept in Bultmann's thought).[12] The study has been described as a classic example of how thoroughly one man can be *mis*-understood by another, and it should be obvious from a careful reading that the description is not unfair. More than once Barth's brilliance led him to get hold of the wrong end of the stick and then to refuse to let go of it but to trace fantastic patterns with it in the air.

Barth could never quite avoid a touch of magisterial hauteur every now and then, a trace of self-importance, even in some of his more self-depreciatory statements, but this and his misuse of wit are no more than inevitable human failings. Ten times more frequent is his good-humoured wit, the brilliant remark which is just the right thing to say at a particular moment and without any overtones to it. Barth's books offer countless examples, but one characteristic instance is worth repeating here. Barth was once introduced to a man on the street. 'Do you know the great theologian?', the man asked. 'Know him?', replied Barth, 'I shave him every morning!'[13] Towards the end of his life, when he turned this wit on himself, it acquired a rather more wistful tinge – mild and gentle, with an autumnal serenity.

Wit, however, is only the beginning. On closer acquaintance with Barth something much less superficial emerges.

That is how much Barth is in love with his subject and how much it brings him a delight that suffuses him with an inner joy. For all his strictness and self-imposed discipline, there is no hint that Barth feels that he is labouring under a heavy burden. For the last half of his life, from about his fortieth birthday onwards, he radiates joy in passages which hardly seem to fit the conventional picture of the continental theologian at work. One such passage is right at the beginning of Barth's own favourite among his books, but also his most difficult work, a study of the argument for the existence of God put forward by the eleventh-century Archbishop of Canterbury, Anselm. The title contains a Latin phrase from Anselm's work, '*Fides Quaerens Intellectum*' (faith seeking understanding). Barth begins by writing about the nature of the faith that looks for understanding, and then goes on to describe what happens as understanding is achieved. As understanding is achieved, it issues – in joy. 'The dominating factor in Anselm's mind is that even the Church Fathers wrote about understanding in order to give the faithful joy in believing by a demonstration of the reason of their faith.'[14] In another passage, Barth locates joy at the centre of all his theology, in the person of God. God is not only gracious and merciful and patient, holy and righteous and wise, free, omnipresent, constant, omnipotent, eternal, he is not only love, but also joy. And because he is joy, it is 'possible, necessary and permissible to have joy in him and before him'.

The special element to be noted and considered is that the glory of God is not only great and sublime or holy and gracious, the overflowing of the sovereignty in which God is love. In all this it is a glory that awakens joy and is itself joyful. It is not merely a glory which is solemn and good and true, and which, in its perfection and sublimity, might be gloomy or at least joyless. Joy in and before God – in its particular nature, distinct from what we mean by awe, gratitude and the rest – has an objective basis. It is something in God,

22

the God of all the perfections, which justifies us in having joy, desire and pleasure towards him, which indeed obliges, summons and attracts us to do this.[15]

Whatever we may think that passage does or does not tell us about God, it certainly tells us a good deal about Karl Barth.

It is only necessary to turn to the original setting of the passage which has just been quoted to discover two further characteristics of Barth and his writing. First, there is the fine sense of structure which holds his work together, and second, the real beauty of the writing itself. Barth's remarks on the joy of God appear in a section of the *Church Dogmatics* entitled 'The Perfections of the Divine Freedom'. The section is divided into three subsections, 'The Unity and Omnipresence of God', 'The Constancy and Omnipotence of God' and 'The Eternity and Glory of God', and each subsection in turn has a shape of its own, as Barth approaches his theme now from one perspective and now from another. Here the structure is on a vast scale, but the same impression is given by even the most miniature of his pieces. Whether it is a long stretch of systematic thinking or a short sermon or an autobiographical article for a journal, the piece is conceived as a whole, so that as one reads it is possible to sense and enjoy the magnificent craftsmanship that has been employed. Translation into English takes away a good deal of the impact of the writing supported by this structure, but even so it can be extremely moving, almost rhapsodic in its tone.

Several analogies have been used to sum up Barth's style. He has been seen as an architect, building on a mediaeval scale and with a mediaeval freedom that is not afraid of inconsistency. He has been seen as a poet or a painter, setting down what has escaped less penetrating eyes. And probably most appropriately of all, he has been compared

23

to the great musicians. One friend described him in terms of Beethoven, as a creative artist who can time and again produce surprises, while keeping them within a coherent structure:

> You feel, 'He cannot do that. This is something illogical, a new theme that interrupts the symphony, that contradicts what we have just been hearing.' And then before you have recovered from your surprise, you discover that with great profundity he has worked it into the texture of the whole symphony and that far from being alien to the main theme it is perfectly integrated with it and wonderfully enriches it. Only a great genius can do that.[16]

'Symphonic' is a good adjective for Barth. There are many kinds of symphony, and one could have an entertaining time relating them to what he has written: in later years the massive and measured paragraphs of Bruckner or the later Beethoven; in an earlier period the demonic energy of Berlioz or a Mahler scherzo; every now and then a piece with all the grace and profundity of Mozart himself.

That, however, is only to skate the surface. The long hours in the study were not spent polishing style. It is important to have seen something of Barth himself and the often unacknowledged attractiveness of his personality and his books, but Barth himself would be the first to admit that his own personality and way of writing were quite secondary. What he was like, how he put what he had to say were immaterial in the face of the question whether what he saw was right, and whether he communicated his vision faithfully.

NOTES

1. As told by Mrs Barth to Ved Mehta, *The New Theologian*, Weidenfeld & Nicolson 1965, p. 108.
2. Karl Barth, *Church Dogmatics* (= *CD*) III 2, T. & T. Clark 1960, p. xi.
3. *CD* IV 4, p. vii.

4. Compiled by Charlotte von Kirschbaum, *Antwort: Karl Barth zum siebzigsten Geburtstag an 10. Mai 1956 dargebracht*, EVZ Verlag, Zurich 1956.

5. In James D. Smart (ed.), *Revolutionary Theology in the Making* (=*RTM*), Epworth Press 1964, pp. 92f.

6. Karl Barth, *The Word of God and the Word of Man* (=*WGWM*), Harper Torchbooks 1957, p. 1.

7. Karl Barth, *Deliverance to the Captives*, SCM Press 1961, pp. 7f.

8. Philip Toynbee, 'The "Tender" Reactionary', *The Observer*, 15 December 1968.

9. Agnes von Zahan-Harnack, *Adolf von Harnack*, Hans Bott Verlag, Berlin 1936, p. 533.

10. Karl Barth, *How I Changed My Mind* (=*HCM*), ed. John D. Godsey, Saint Andrew Press 1969, pp. 7, 15, 16, 34–36, 73, 74.

11. Dietrich Bonhoeffer, *No Rusty Swords*, ed. E. H. Robertson, Collins 1965, p. 121.

12. In H. W. Bartsch (ed.), *Kerygma and Myth* II, SPCK 1962, pp. 83–132.

13. *HCM*, p. 14.

14. Karl Barth, *Anselm: Fides Quaerens Intellectum*, SCM Press 1960, p. 15.

15. *CD* II 1, p. 655.

16. T. F. Torrance, *Karl Barth: An Introduction to his Early Theology: 1910–1931* (=*TFT*), SCM Press 1962, p. 23.

2 Prophet

Karl Barth's greatness was that he brought to twentieth-century Christian thinking a towering conception of God which had long been lost. This new conception of God came to him because he rediscovered the Bible. And he rediscovered the Bible because he had to preach from it Sunday by Sunday to a congregation in a small Swiss town. So the story of Barth begins in the pulpit at Safenwil, a small community in one of the valleys in the north-east of Switzerland, on the main road and railway line from Olten to Aarau, set in predominantly farming country but with two or three local industries which provided employment for its inhabitants. It was Barth's first parish, and he was there for almost ten years between his twenty-fifth and thirty-fifth birthdays, from 1912 to 1921.

There is nothing special about Safenwil, and there was nothing special about Barth, when he arrived there, to mark him out from the thousands of other pastors who had faced a similar situation in the Swiss Reformed Church. The one crucial difference ultimately proved to be that Barth took the work of preaching with the utmost seriousness, and with his penetrating mind pursued the problems it presented until he arrived at what for him was the only possible solution.

'Why do people come to church?' he asked himself. To satisfy an old habit? To be entertained and instructed? To be edified? What makes people leave their work or their homes, the possibility of enjoying themselves in the open air, to go into a church building when the bells begin to ring? They expect something. They are looking for the presence of God. But how are they to find God? How is he present? Certainly not as when divine presence is sensed in the beauties of nature, of music and the arts, of personal relationships. *If* God is present in church, he must be present in the forms of praying and singing, of reading and hearing the Bible, of preaching.[1]

Preaching, above all, is the way in which God is brought to a particular congregation on a particular Sunday morning. If that is so, however, can the preacher be adequate to the task that is set him? The preacher is a man; he may be trained, he may be experienced, he may be well read – but he is still a man, and he has to speak the word of God. The people have come to hear, not his opinions on some great political or religious issue, but what God himself has to say to them.

Barth sees the task of the preacher in these exalted terms because of the tradition of the church to which he belongs. For the Swiss Reformed Church the sermon occupied the centre of the service much in the same way as the Catholic mass centres on the eucharistic action. From his earliest days he was fascinated by the sense of miracle in Catholic services, the feeling of action and event which takes place regardless of outward circumstances. He spoke with some envy of the group of Benedictines chanting the Magnificat in their chapel when it was hit by a French shell: 'The smoke thinned away and the Magnificat continued. I ask you whether a Protestant sermon would have been continued.' Roman Catholics go to church for the saving radiance of the eucharistic miracle, yet the Reformation expected to see something better. 'The visible Word, the objectively clarified preaching of the Word, is the only

27

sacrament left to us. The Reformers sternly took from us everything but the Bible.'[2]

So it was in the Bible that Barth began to look for the solution to his problem of how a man could speak the word of God to his congregation. What he found there burst upon him like a completely new discovery. This may seem strange; ought one not to expect a preacher to be familiar with the Bible? But as we shall see, university education at that time and the current trend of theology tended to obscure much of the content of the Bible. The Old Testament was in process of being written off; the New Testament was little more than 'a handbook of comparative religion for the comparatively religious'.

As Barth read the Bible, he reported on what he found with all the enthusiasm and wonderment of a traveller who has just come back from a strange new land. Open the Bible, he asks, and what do we find? We stand with Abraham in Haran and hear a promise; we stand with Moses in the wilderness and hear a command; we stand with Gideon by the oak at Ophrah and we see an angelic vision; we lie with Samuel at the tabernacle at Shiloh and hear a voice. What does it all mean? We follow the message of the prophets, we read the pity, the hope and confidence of the psalms, and then, much later, we come to that figure who was no prophet, no poet, no hero, no thinker, yet all of these and more, with his triumphant cry, 'I am the resurrection and the life.' We find this cry echoed, in different ways, in the letters of Paul and John, and then the echo dies away. We have come to the end of the Bible.[3]

What is it all about? What are these witnesses trying to say? The Bible is about history – that runs through all its pages. It is also about morality – it has countless illustrations of virtue and human greatness. And it is about religion – ways of thinking about God and conducting oneself in his

28

presence. All these things are there. But the Bible is about something more. As we read the Bible, we have the same experience as that of the first martyr, Stephen: 'I see the heavens opened, and the Son of man standing on the right hand of God.' This does not happen to us of our own skill and our own deserving; but if we entrust ourselves to the Bible and come to grips with it, it takes us in its grip, meets us, guides us and draws us on.

> It is not the right human thoughts about God which form the content of the Bible, but the right divine thoughts about men. The Bible tells us not how we should talk with God but what he says to us; not how we find the way to him, but how he has sought and found the way to us; not the right relation in which we must place ourselves to him, but the covenant which he has made with all who are Abraham's spiritual children and which he has sealed once and for all in Jesus Christ. It is this which is within the Bible. The word of God is within the Bible.[4]

So the people of Safenwil listened to sermons of a quite unprecedented kind, sermons not only deeply rooted in the Bible but also blazing with a passionate ardour, sermons deliberately emphasizing the gulf between Barth's discovery and the conventional wisdom of the time. Certainly they would never have heard a commentary on the meeting between Nicodemus and Jesus in the Gospel of John like that given by Barth. Nicodemus arrives, Barth explains, with the intention of leading a cautious, judicious, tolerant, religious conversation as from one bank of a stream to the other. 'Rabbi, we know that you are a teacher come from God.' But he has scarcely opened his mouth when he is stopped. 'Truly I say to you, unless a man is born again he cannot see the kingdom of God.' All Nicodemus' cards are struck from his hand and he finds himself face to face with something incomprehensible, something he cannot fathom. 'How can a man be born again when he is old?' This is no talk from shore to shore; Nicodemus is suddenly in the middle of the stream with the ground taken from under his feet. He cannot take a position of his own nor engage in a genuine exchange of opinions. The time for tolerance is past; a choice has to be made: 'Either-or'. 'Unless a man is born of water and the spirit, he cannot enter the kingdom of God.' Nicodemus stammers, 'How can these things be?' Jesus answers, 'Are you a teacher of Israel and do not understand these things?' Nicodemus is checkmated in three moves.[5]

There is much of Nicodemus in the theology that Barth was taught in his university days; not least, he is arguing with his former background and something of his former self. So we are taken back to the end of the nineteenth century, and the path by which Barth came to arrive at Safenwil.[6]

Karl Barth had theology in his very blood. His grandparents on both sides had been ministers in the Reformed Church and when Karl was born, on 10 May 1886, his father was teaching at the Evangelical School of Preachers in Basel. Fritz Barth was theologically a conservative, but was one of the more progressive members of the church to which he belonged. When Karl was three, he moved to Bern, to become first lecturer and then professor in church history and New Testament exegesis. He wrote a by no means insignificant *Introduction to the New Testament*.

Looking back on his childhood, Karl picked out the time of his confirmation as the real beginning of his own vocation to theology. 'On the eve of my confirmation day,' he wrote, 'I boldly resolved to become a theologian, perhaps not so much with the thought of preaching, cure of souls and the like, but rather in the hope of realizing in the course of this study some substantial understanding of a confession of faith of which I had only a vague apprehension.'[7] Like all

30

young Swiss men, he was also involved at that time in compulsory military training which he found not at all distasteful. The man who was to spring many surprises on his friends throughout his life about the range of his interests was, as a boy, fascinated with military tactics and played endless games of toy soldiers with his two brothers, Peter and Heinrich; perhaps prophetically, his favourite role was that of Napoleon.

Once Karl's chosen career became evident, his father tried to exercise a guiding hand in his choice of university and Karl to begin with did his best to comply. His five years of university study began in Bern, under the direction of his father, where he received a solid diet of Reformed theology. However, towards the end of his second year he came up against two new influences: the theoretical and practical philosophy of the idealist Immanuel Kant, author of a 'Copernican revolution' in the theory of knowledge at the end of the eighteenth century, and the analysis of religion and faith made by the theologian Friedrich Schleiermacher, who was to dominate German theology for a century after his death in 1834. As a result, Karl expressed a desire to go to Marburg, in Germany, to study under the leading Kantian theologian of the day, Wilhelm Herrmann. This move was opposed by his father, and eventually a compromise was reached: Karl moved to Berlin for a semester, to be taught by Adolf von Harnack, the greatest liberal church historian of his generation. So involved did Karl become in his work there, that it is reported that he saw next to nothing of the German capital during his stay, a striking contrast to his confessed idleness in Bern.

It was accepted that the student would attend a variety of universities before completing his training, so further moves were quite in order. Karl's third year was completed at Bern, but in 1907 he enrolled at the University of

31

Tübingen to hear the lectures of the conservative New Testament theologian, Adolf Schlatter, again his father's choice. Filial duty having at last been done, however, Karl felt free to go to Marburg, a university which, in addition to his idol, Herrmann, contained many of the leading German New Testament scholars and philosophers. There he remained for a whole year, until it was time to return to Bern and take his final examinations.

Further study for a doctorate and an academic career were never in question at this stage, so ordination and the pastoral ministry were the next logical steps. Karl was in fact ordained by the church in Bern in 1908, after his examinations, but two serious difficulties stood in the way of an immediate start to pastoral work. The first problem was the nature of the particular theology which appealed most to him at the time. Herrmann's theology, which had proved such an attraction, was very much a theology of human experience and particularly of the human conscience. The ground of faith was man's innate moral sense, the still small voice inside him, which was aroused by the impact of Jesus, his life and teaching. Contact with Jesus, the perfect religious personality, nourished a man's own religious experience and contributed to his religious growth. To be an honest exponent of this theology, Barth believed, he had to share its fundamental conviction and bring to it the necessary depth of experience. But this he was unable to do, and he was too honest to go on as he was.

The second difficulty was more widespread, and consisted in the simple fact that university theological education, especially in the more liberal universities (of which Marburg was a leading example), then seemed calculated to make men less rather than more fitted to embark on the pastoral ministry. The problem was felt not only by the students themselves but also by some of the more thoughtful of their teachers, among them figures like the Old Testament scholar Julius Wellhausen and the systematic theologian Ernst Troeltsch, each of whom asked to be transferred from the faculty of theology elsewhere. The very nature and indeed the possibility of theology at all were much in question. It was the hey-day of the sciences, and their progress seemed to make the question of God and traditional religious belief more and more problematical. Study began, as a matter of course, from the human end, from a scientific approach to the natural world and to human experience, and all the roads from there to assertions about God were cluttered with a variety of traffic. Religion and culture, theology and history, fused into one. Man seemed increasingly to be the master of his destiny. It was felt that his capacity for achieving beauty, attaining truth, perfecting his own nature, was growing all the time, and Christianity served as a religious endorsement of the general trend. It was presented as a general belief in the fatherhood of God and the brotherhood of man, with Jesus as little more than a prophet of divine goodwill. In this context Herrmann's theology was a better example than many, but it was still coloured by its background.[8]

It would be wrong to paint the situation in too negative terms; among all this activity were some developments quite essential for the healthy progress of the understanding of the Christian tradition, however much they were linked with more undesirable elements. For example, during this period the historical and literary criticism of the Bible took giant strides forward, using techniques which even Barth himself was not to question. But this work was, from the pastoral point of view, negative more than positive; it was useful for a student who was critical of the tradition in which he found himself, but it was no basis for parish work.

So there was a wait, and for a year Barth returned to

Marburg as an editorial assistant on the staff of the leading popular liberal theological journal, *The Christian World*. This period over, he took the final step and went to Geneva as assistant minister to the German-speaking congregation there. His views were still very much the theology that he had learned at the university and with *The Christian World*, but he was far from happy with it, and when he moved from there to Safenwil his problems had by no means been resolved.

In addition to his positive discovery of the content of the Bible it was finally a negative discovery that led Barth to sever most of his links with the past and to resolve his dilemma in the direction which he eventually followed. Two years after his arrival at Safenwil, the First World War broke out. A few days after it was declared, a document known as the 'Manifesto of the Intellectuals' appeared, signed by ninety-three scholars and artists, supporting the war policy of the Kaiser. Barth looked at the signatures appended to it. To his horror, they included the names of the most prominent of the teachers under whom he had studied: Harnack, Schlatter, even Herrmann. This, then, was the consequence of their theology and their ethics, their understanding of the Bible and of history. If that was what the great cultural synthesis, in the climate of which Barth had been brought up, meant in practical terms, then there was no point in following the road any further. It was time for something new.[9]

Other people play relatively little part in Barth's life. Certainly he showed great interest in those who talked with him; a British acquaintance spoke of his 'pastoral' style.[10] Yet all the evidence is that he was always bound up in the world of ideas and principles far more than with human lives. At any rate, few of his friends from the early days remained friends until his old age, though a surprising number of them proved to be as long-lived as Barth himself. That makes it all the more important to record two particularly close relationships that began at Safenwil, and continued to the end of Barth's days. In his second year he married Nelly Hoffmann, an attractive young violinist, with whom he celebrated a better than golden wedding anniversary. Like many a *Hausfrau* in the German tradition, her place was very much in the background, but the fact that she hardly appears in this account is certainly not to minimize her importance: she lived to survive her husband and bore him four sons (two became theologians, one is a landscape architect and one was killed in a climbing accident) and a daughter.

In the same year, a friend from Barth's Marburg days became pastor at Leutwil, another small village over the mountains to the south. His name was Eduard Thurneysen and he became Barth's bosom companion. The two men met regularly, and when they were unable to meet corresponded by letter and postcard; it is this informal correspondence that illuminates Barth's one period of parish work.[11]

Barth must have made a strange pastor. He was acutely conscious of the characteristics that marked him out from his fellow-clergy and regularly expressed his feeling of inadequacy for the work that had been committed to him. He was worried that he was unable to be 'a pastor that pleases the people',[12] and he apologized publicly to his people as he left the parish that they had had to put up with a pastor who lived in his study.[13] Years afterwards, at the very end of his career, when he summed up his thoughts on the nature and purpose of theology in a final series of lectures, he spoke of the solitude with which the theologian is so often burdened. In his words one can surely trace the memory of early experience at Safenwil:

We might think, above all, of the especially pathetic figure of the pastor in his solitude – his solitary pathway and the uncanny isolation, which, due to the priestly halo which he is still thought to wear, continue to characterize him. He remains a stranger among all the men of his urban and rural community; at best he may be surrounded by a small circle of those who feel particularly concerned. Scarcely anyone (with the exception of one or another colleague who is not geographically or doctrinally too remote from him) can offer him a helping hand in the labour demanded of him, in the explication and application of the biblical message, and in his own theological work.[14]

Whatever his feelings and his capabilities, however, he certainly tried. His correspondence with Thurneysen offers a series of vignettes of parish life and his reactions to it. The small factories of Safenwil provided their own industrial problems in the form of friction between workers and management. Barth was an ardent social democrat and took the side of the workers, an action which earned him the nickname of 'the red pastor'. He compares himself to Moses before Pharaoh as he goes up to have a heart-to-heart talk at the villa of the local manufacturer who has threatened to sack fifty-five women in the knitting mill because they organized themselves into a union.[15] Shortly after the war he writes that he recently awoke as president of an eleven-member emergency commission to cope with the aftermath and the influenza epidemic.[16] He works conscientiously, but without enthusiasm: 'simply because it is necessary'.[17] Secretly he wishes that it was possible to abandon the regularly recurring confirmation classes, but that does not prevent him from making the most of them if they have to be held: 'Yesterday I had a great snowball fight with the boys of my confirmation class. I do that for them every year in order to improve the general joyousness.'[18]

It is the church itself that proves the greatest burden. 'Forget you are in church,' he tells the congregation. 'Forget that a minister stands before you. The church is a great,

36

perhaps the greatest hindrance to repentance. If we wish to hear the call of Jesus, we must hear it despite the church.'[19] He has no time for church committees, for clergy meetings and administration; his one thought is of the easiest way to dissociate himself from them with a clear conscience. Yet again, he cannot abandon the church.[20]

However much a man may be tempted to dislike the Church and to pour scorn upon it, he will never entertain the idea of leaving it or of renouncing his orders, for that would be even less intelligent than if he were to take his own life. He knows the catastrophe of the Church to be inevitable; and he knows also that there is no friendly lifeboat into which he can clamber and row clear of the imminent disaster. He knows that he must remain at his post in the engine-room or, maybe, on the bridge. . . . Attacks on the Church which proceed upon the assumption that its enemies possess some superior knowledge or some superior method of justifying and saving themselves are – non-sense. Consequently, when the prophet raises his voice to preserve the memory of eternity in himself and in the Church, he will always prefer to take up his position in hell with the Church than to exalt himself into a heaven which does not exist.[21]

Despite his remoteness, Barth left behind him at Safenwil a group of people who, forty years later, still remembered their one-time pastor with affection.[22] They may not have understood what he said; they may have talked a good deal about his oddities while he was among them, but like country people elsewhere, they had the shrewdness to recognize a notable man when they saw him. One incident above all indicates Barth's sympathy for his people as well as his strength, and shows that what he understood by preaching was very different from the hard line presented by the evangelicals of his time. It was when the visiting evangelist arrived for a whole week of mission preaching.

Barth went every night to listen. He described what he heard as 'a bad form of religious mechanics'; it was psychologizing at its worst, just a describing of 'Christian' spiritual experiences: 'here an awakening, a conversion, a sealing,

37

then five different levels of resistance to the Holy Spirit, then the blood of Christ flows as medicine for the soul, and finally everything comes to a climax in the appeal to the "awakened" (*a*) to visit an after-meeting in the chapel, (*b*) to pray frequently on their knees, (*c*) to buy a little book, (*d*) to subscribe to the magazine *Tabernacle Greeting*.' The preacher continually pointed to the open jaws of hell into which a man could disappear in spite of all these splendours. And over it, Barth remarked, there brooded an atmosphere of fear as though the ship were sinking and there was no lifeboat for most people, although the music was playing 'Nearer my God, to Thee' with might and main.

So it went on until Sunday at last came and Barth awoke with the drowsy, yet happy thought, 'Now it's my turn.' And what theme did he choose? 'In contrast to all the soul experiences and gruesome thundering about sin, I asserted calmly that there is joy with God (e.g. little angels with harps and sheets of music) and that the kingdom of God on earth begins with joy.'[23]

Little angels with harps and sheets of music! That was not the tone in which he was now to make his mark on the outside world. Rather, he was credited with a bombshell, an earthquake, a volcano, a thunderbolt. Barth himself described the disturbance he was now to create in the theological world by comparing himself to someone groping his way up the stairs in a dark church tower and clutching at the handrail for support. Instead, he has hold of the bell rope, and suddenly to his horror hears the great bell ringing out above him.[24]

What happened was this. In his rediscovery of the Bible, Barth rediscovered Paul, and, like others before him, fell captive to the Epistle to the Romans. With the aid of every

38

relevant book he could find he worked right through the text, trying to bring out its innermost meaning. His correspondence with Thurneysen records his progress: chapter 3 in September 1916, chapter 5 in September 1917, chapter 9 by March 1918 and the work completed and the preface written, to time, in August of the same year.[25] The work served as a focal point for all his concerns; philosophical idealism, romanticism, religious socialism, biblical thought, the experience of the war are all caught up with Paul's own words to drive home the fact that the world of man is corrupted by sin and that his attempts to assert himself without God, even by religion or piety, are useless. Salvation comes only as God's gift and his kingdom must break into the present age before man can play his part in bringing about its fulfilment. A Swiss publisher had become interested in the book in its later stages and printed a small edition of one thousand copies. It met with moderate success; only three hundred copies were sold in Barth's native Switzerland, but there was a wider market in the turmoil of postwar Germany. Flashpoint had not quite been reached.

It was the second edition that triggered off the real explosion. Looking back on what he had written scarcely a year after it had been published Barth found it 'overloaded and bloated' everywhere; he could not bear the thought of a possible reprint, and decided that it had to be 'reformed root and branch', much to the dismay of his publisher.[26] Not for the last time, he sat down and worked over the same ground once again. From this second attempt emerged the most powerful piece of theological writing of the twentieth century. The revision took a year's concentrated work, often rewriting passages two or three times to get them right; Barth compared himself to an old potter whom he once saw working inside a furnace so that only his shoes stuck out: 'I amble like a drunk man back and forth between writing desk, dining table and bed, travelling each kilometre with my eye on the next one: there was something that, between two and three in the morning, would not come out right.'[27]

The final result of these labours is ultimately indescribable; it has to be read at first hand for its full impact to be felt, and though the reader is unlikely to have the stamina to survive five hundred pages of sustained assault at the first attempt, he will not come away from even a brief reading without being affected in one way or the other. The opening of Barth's comments on Romans 9 gives some indication of what is to be expected:

God, the pure and absolute boundary and beginning of all that we are and have and do; God, who is distinguished qualitatively from men and from everything human, and must never be identified with anything which we name, or experience, or conceive, or worship, as God; God, who confronts all human disturbance with an unconditional command 'Halt', and all human rest with an equally unconditional command 'Advance'; God, the 'Yes' in our 'No' and the 'No' in our 'Yes', the First and the Last, and, consequently, the Unknown, who is never a known thing in the midst of other known things; God, the Lord, the Creator, the Redeemer – this is the Living God. In the Gospel, in the Message of Salvation of Jesus Christ, this Hidden, Living, God has revealed Himself, as He is. Above and beyond the apparently infinite series of possibilities and visibilities in this world there breaks forth, like a flash of lightning, impossibility and invisibility, not as some separate, second, other thing, but as the Truth of God which is now hidden, as the Primal Origin to which all things are related, as the dissolution of all relativity, and therefore as the reality of all relative realities. Though – nay rather, because – human life is temporal, finite, and passing to corruption, it is revealed in the Gospel that the glorious, triumphant, existential inevitability of the Kingdom of God cannot be hidden. It is made manifest that the knowledge of God – faith working through love – is presented to men as the possibility which, though realized at no particular moment in time, is, nevertheless, open to them at every moment, as the new and realizable possibility of their being what they are in God – His children – cast, as men of this world, under judgment, looking for righteousness and awaiting redemption, but, under grace, already liberated.[28]

This paragraph illustrates a number of the characteristic themes of *Romans* as well as Barth's style. First, there is the heaping up of phrases to stress the utter Godness of God, the great gulf that separates him from man – and there is barely a page in the book which does not add to the list. Nothing can bridge this gap from man's side, no one can cross the barrier; nor can the exercise by God of his power be read off from nature or from human history. God is 'the Holy One, the altogether Other'.[29] In face of him, man is absolutely nothing and his achievements are useless; whereas in the first edition of *Romans* Barth allowed man some part in establishing the kingdom of God once it had broken in, now he makes him quite corrupt and helpless. 'The righteousness of God is a vast impossibility; and as such it forms an absolute obstacle to the claim of any human righteousness to be either an anticipation of what will finally be or a relic of what once has been.'[30] Man cannot even contribute his faith. Faith, one of the section headings states, is miracle.[31] It is not revealed to us by flesh and blood; no one can communicate it to himself or to anyone else. 'What I heard yesterday I must hear again to-day; and if I am to hear it afresh to-morrow, it must be revealed by the Father of Jesus, who is in heaven, and by Him only.'[32] It is through Jesus that the union between God and man is achieved, but this Jesus is not the human figure who walked the roads of Palestine and shared human existence. It is hard to find any idea of incarnation in what Barth writes. Jesus is 'the plane that intersects vertically from above', touching the old world of the flesh 'as a tangent touches a circle, that is, without touching it'. 'And yet,' Barth goes on, 'precisely because he does not touch it, he touches it as its frontier.'[33] Such a statement, and the many similar ones in the extended quotation above, is the raw material of Barth's theology. It is *dialectic*, each statement being followed by another statement saying the opposite, for it is only in this tension of opposites, Barth believes, that it is possible to convey what has to be said.[34]

It was a combination of the reading he had done since embarking on the first edition of *Romans* and meetings and conversations with a small group of other like-minded pastors, including now well-known theological names like Gogarten and Brunner, that stimulated Barth to achieve this new climax within so short a time. Partly, of course, it was a result of the climate of that period, the aftermath of the war and its horrors, that led to this gospel of salvation through despair and disgust. But that was only part of the story. There was also, for Barth, the discovery or rediscovery of Dostoievsky and Kierkegaard, of Nietzsche and Nietzsche's friend the Swiss sceptic Overbeck, together with the recently published study by Rudolf Otto, *The Idea of the Holy*. Above all, however, there was the Bible itself, and continued reading of Paul himself.[35]

What sort of a book is this theological dynamite? How much of its foundation, Paul's own Epistle to the Romans, is preserved in the finished structure? Barth compared himself with the Reformer Calvin, who, once he had established what stood in the text, set himself to rethink the whole material and to wrestle with it, till the walls separating the sixteenth century from the first became transparent.[36] This would seem to be very near the mark. A recent study of Calvin's interpretative method seems very reminiscent of Barth:

We almost forget which century we are in; we hardly know whether the participants are *they* or *we*. We are talking about the Judaizers in Galatia – no, we are not, they are the Romanists in France and Switzerland – indeed, we are not talking about the Judaizers at all, we are joining in the controversy, we are taking sides, entering into an engagement that will certainly change the outward course of our lives. Or St John is speaking; but as we listen, his Greek strangely

42

becomes the sort of Latin or French with which we are familiar and we find to our surprise that he knows about our modern problems and says the definitive thing about them. In Calvin's commentaries the first and sixteenth centuries are so intertwined that it is often quite impossible to separate them.[37]

But if the method is like that of Calvin, it is taken to far greater extremes; the process is carried out at a far higher temperature, deliberately, so that pressure is raised to bursting point and the explosion inevitably follows. The price that has to be paid as a result is something that we must consider later.

While Barth was rewriting *Romans*, he had other things to think about. In February 1921, much to his surprise, an invitation came to him from the Reformed Church of Eastern Friedland to accept a newly established professorial chair in the University of Göttingen. The offer provided much food for thought; negotiations were slow and Barth was very hesitant about accepting. It was a far cry from the mountains of Switzerland and the peculiarities of Swiss dialect to the flat northern plains of Germany and the comparative purity of High German. Barth would certainly feel a stranger in a very different country. In addition, he was lacking in the necessary qualifications; he had no teaching experience and could not even boast a doctorate to his name. Moreover, it was not even as if he had an established position to go to. Theology at the university was dominantly Lutheran; the new chair had been created, with the help of American money, to make possible the study of Reformed dogmatics; it also bore the description 'Honorary'. (It is worth wondering whether, despite the success of the *Epistle to the Romans* – then only in its first edition – he would have stood any more chance than other gifted country parsons in gaining advancement had it not been for some of these apparent disadvantages!) Barth saw it all: 'Professor,

Systematic Theology, Reformed, Göttingen, Hanover, Germany – every word a question mark. America (the West!) in the background – a great question mark.'[38]

Picturing himself at Göttingen, Barth could see himself as being nothing but a grotesque failure. And yet, how could he refuse the opportunity? He might not seem up to such a move, but on the other hand he was hardly at home in the parish ministry either, 'chewing wearily for twelve years on the one half of the sour theological apple', as he put it in one of his more depressed moods.[39]

So he decided to go. At least one happy event marked the transition to the new life. He did not arrive at Göttingen without a doctorate after all. On 31 January 1922, in the thick of his first year, news arrived that the University of Münster had awarded him an honorary doctorate in theology 'for his contribution to the deepening of the formulation of religious and theological questioning'. Modestly, he celebrated the honour with a small black coffee. His family seemed to be more impressed. His small daughter, like small daughters the world over, managed to find just the right comment to mark the occasion. 'Daddy,' she asked, 'will you now be able to make little children well?'[40]

NOTES

1. *WGWM*, pp. 104ff. 2. *WGWM*, pp. 112ff.
3. *WGWM*, pp. 28ff. 4. *WGWM*, p. 43.
5. Karl Barth and Eduard Thurneysen, *Come Holy Spirit*, T. & T. Clark 1936, pp. 102ff.
6. There are short summaries of Barth's life by John D. Godsey in *HCM*, pp. 9–33; *TFT*, pp. 15–18; A. B. Come, *An Introduction to Barth's Dogmatics for Preachers*, SCM Press 1963, pp. 23–67; see also W. Nicholls, *The Pelican Guide to Modern Theology* I, Penguin Books 1969, pp. 77ff.
7. 'Karl Barth and Oscar Cullmann on their Theological Vocation', *Scottish Journal of Theology*, 1961, p. 225.
8. See especially Karl Barth, 'Evangelical Theology in the Nineteenth Century', in *The Humanity of God*, Fontana Books 1967, pp. 9ff.

9. *The Humanity of God*, pp. 12f.

10. R. Gregor Smith, in Karl Barth, *Against the Stream*, SCM Press 1954, p. 8

11. Collected in *RTM*.   12. *RTM*, p. 22.

13. Karl Barth, *The Epistle to the Romans*, OUP 1933, p. 15.

14. Karl Barth, *Evangelical Theology*, Fontana Books 1965, pp. 105f.

15. *RTM*, p. 42.   16. *RTM*, p. 45.

17. *RTM*, p. 36.   18. *RTM*, p. 28.

19. *Come Holy Spirit*, p. 71.   20. *RTM*, pp. 34f., 37.

21. *Romans*, pp. 336f.   22. *RTM*, p. 22.

23. *RTM*, pp. 39f.

24. Karl Barth, *Die Christliche Dogmatik im Entwurf*, Christian Kaiser Verlag, Munich 1927, p. ix.

25. *RTM*, pp. 38, 42, 43, 44; *Romans*, p. 2.

26. *RTM*, p. 55.   27. *RTM*, p. 59.

28. *Romans*, pp. 330–332.   29. *Romans*, p. 82.

30. *Romans*, pp. 108f.   31. *Romans*, pp. 125–131.

32. *Romans*, p. 98.   33. *Romans*, p. 30.

34. *Romans*, p. 261.   35. *Romans*, pp. 3f.

36. *Romans*, p. 7.

37. T. H. L. Parker, *Calvin's New Testament Commentaries*, SCM Press 1971, pp. 91f.

38. *RTM*, p. 56.   39. *RTM*, p. 58.

40. *RTM*, p. 61.

3 Professor

In his first, sympathetic letters to Göttingen, Eduard Thurney-sen imagined the worst – the strangeness, the loneliness of his friend, the remoteness from home.[1] But he need not have worried. Barth's replies reassured him. There was far too much work to do for him to have time to reflect on his position. For any teacher the first term is always by far the worst, and Barth had more to work out than most. He could not for ever lecture on the Epistle to the Romans, yet on the other hand after *Romans* there was neither the possibility of nor the inclination for a more conventional lecture programme. In the blinding new light in which he saw the nature and purpose of theology, Barth wanted to look more closely at those parts of the Christian tradition that were so far unfamiliar to him, as well as to continue to study the writers who, whether positively or negatively, had given him so much. He therefore devoted himself to exposition and criticism of other writers rather than launching out on his own: he pressed on with study of the Epistle to the Ephesians and I Corinthians, and added to this lectures on Schleier-macher, the Reformers and some of the Reformed confessions.[2]

There seemed almost too much to get through. 'If only someone would give me time, time, time, to do everything properly, to read everything at my own tempo, to take it apart and put it together again', he wrote to his friends in a circular letter. And he warned them, 'like the rich man in hell', not to let a single hour pass fruitlessly in the rectory or reading the newspaper, as had happened to him at Safenwil. 'You, too, may one day become professors, and then with what rage will you regard each book that you did not read or did not read in such a way as really to know the how and wherefore of it.'[3]

It would all have been very much easier if the university had not been full of students. Barth was hardly an uncontroversial figure, and as he lectured, he came up against considerable opposition as well as causing some excitement. Students clamoured to see him and to argue with him:

> After an aggressive lecture yesterday, the whole afternoon was spent walking with seven men on the Nikolausberg, during which time I had to answer question after question without a break: Sir, what do you think of . . . ? How do you know that . . . ? What do you mean when . . . ? It is hard work until from time to time they are all quiet again, at least for now, and have what they want to know. But tomorrow they are there again. What are tomorrow's two discussion periods likely to produce? And on Wednesday the open evening? And on Thursday the 'Schlüchtern youth' who have made a special appointment? This activity I never really expected, and I wonder also whether it can and should continue and for how long?[4]

For a while, Barth considered discontinuing some of his more informal times with the students, but he never actually took the step. As at Safenwil, he was never less than conscientious, even when he found the work a burden. Indeed, his record of contacts with students throughout his life was considerably better than that of the average German professor. From the start he held open evenings, at which a variety of study activities were tried. One year he had those who came reading aloud from theological works (not as pointless an activity as it might seem), and another he allowed them to write short papers on any subject of their choice.[5]

He made his mark, but amidst a variety of frustrations.

47

For one who always lectured from a fully written-out text, the burden of preparation was fiendish. 'More than once what I presented at 7 a.m. was not ready until between 3 and 5 a.m.'[6] He went on to comment wryly that it was bearable only because it was presented in a menacingly impressive voice.[7] And there were even limits to the use of that. Lecturing was not preaching, and the more subdued tone was difficult to adjust to after ten years. 'At most once in the hour, or not even that, the finger is raised and "Gentlemen!" rings out to introduce a direct word.'[8] He did preach occasionally, but not as often as he would have liked, and even the extended tours which he was able to make through Germany during the vacations, lecturing and preaching to numerous church groups, did not make up for the constraint on the message with which he was still burning. 'Never to break out! Never to work with "God is God"! Never to preach! Never to give expression to the triviality that fills one if he does not do that!'[9]

Yet there was much to be satisfied with. He may have felt repressed, on the treadmill, inferior, 'like the wandering gypsy with only a couple of leaky kettles to call his own, but who in compensation occasionally sets a house on fire',[10] but the students did come to listen, and in a voluntary system of enrolment, that was some sign of success. It may even have led to the envy of other professors who thought and acted so *very* differently. Whether or not this happened, his colleagues often gave Barth a very difficult time. There was a considerable battle to be fought if Barth was to get anywhere in a university context. For while he himself might have changed out of all recognition in the fifteen years since he had left the university, German universities had not. The World War might have taken its huge toll of lives, bringing depression and great hardship in its wake, the social order might be collapsing, with inflation raging furiously and

48

winters bringing purgatorial cruelty, but German theology was relatively little changed, and some of the figures who had dominated it in pre-war days were still very much in circulation and dictated its climate.

The continued correspondence with Thurneysen indicates several occasions on which there were minor clashes between Barth and his colleagues, but the root cause of the on-going arguments is illustrated much more clearly by a public dispute in which Barth was engaged for a number of years, with his old teacher from Berlin days, Adolf von Harnack.

Barth's new-found direction brought him into head-on conflict with Harnack, still as influential as any theologian in Germany, from an early stage. Harnack, with the mellowness of old age (he celebrated his seventieth birthday in 1922) seems to have exercised considerable tolerance towards the fiery Barth; as the dispute goes its way his comments and arguments are always courteous, and as much as anything else reflect a real puzzlement.[11] At one stage he wrote to a friend *à propos* of Barth's theology that he had never thought that a theological speculation could emerge for which he had no antenna. In private correspondence with Harnack, Barth reciprocated the courtesy; in at attempt at reassurance he wrote to Harnack of the constant awareness of the historical and material relativity necessarily attaching to his theology which oppressed him day and night. Even supposing that this awareness had been lacking, his translation into the 'insidious academic sphere' would have made quite certain that the trees did not grow up to heaven, even in his dreams.[12]

A rather different attitude, however, is reflected in Barth's communications with Thurneysen. They are allies in a cause whose progress against all that Harnack stands for is described in highly-coloured naval terms: battleships are

49

brought up to silence the torpedo boats and cruisers that prove such a pest.[13] To Thurneysen, Barth writes in a more mocking tone. He quotes an attractively written card to himself from Harnack, only to make fun of it, and draws a scathing picture of a visit to a house where Harnack was staying:

> I went with bold step to Eberhard Vischer's, and asked for Harnack. There I burst into the midst of a great gathering in which (as I later heard in a roundabout way) they had just been disposing of me. Harnack was enthroned on a settee, was addressed as 'Your excellency', and dispensed bon mots ('Two things are international: money and the spirit', and such like). Afterwards there was an hour-long interview with him and Eberhard Vischer. I asked him what he understood by 'profane' and heard from him that he meant the one-sidedness practised by me, that does injury to the mystery of God. He could not give such a smooth answer to my next question, which was whether he did not have to grant at least the historical (NT) validity of my position. Both gentlemen entangled themselves until they asserted that the forgiveness of sins is something quite simple which belongs merely to the love of neighbour and which he, Harnack, exercises continually. It may be desirable that the church should be shaken *a bit*, but I do my best to keep my conception of God to myself and not make an 'export article' of it. Finally I was branded a Calvinist and intellectualist and let go with the prophecy that according to all the experiences of church history I will found a sect and receive inspirations.[14]

What was in dispute can readily be guessed. For Harnack, after the war as before, there was still some link between religion and culture, between God and the good, the true and the beautiful; for Barth, the gospel had as much or as little to do with culture as with barbarianism.[15] Again, Harnack was deeply concerned with understanding the gospel and making it understandable; his aim was 'not to say the commonplace with uncommon words but to say the uncommon with common words',[16] and he feared that if Barth's approach won the day, theology would fall into the hands of revivalist propagandists who would create their own understanding of the Bible and set up their own authority. Barth, in writing and speaking as he did, was all too aware that the uncommon cannot be conveyed in any way that men might be able to call common. Only a new style could convey the overpowering new reality that he saw. The two men never made real contact. The whole of their argument is an exercise in non-communication. There was far more than a generation gap in the way.

It is common to dismiss Harnack as a faded old liberal who did not grasp the significance of what was happening, to throw back in his face his liberal optimism and his too ready identification with German state policy at the beginning of the First World War. Yet a careful reading of what was said will show that Harnack had more perception than he is often credited with, and that in fact he had the last word in a dispute which, far from being a period piece, is more than ever relevant today. Did Barth, he asked, have no thought for those who, whether theologians or ordinary people, were unable to tread the difficult path that he himself had chosen? Was this really the only way to salvation? Ought not Barth perhaps to realize that while he was playing his instruments, God had other instruments to play as well?[17]

If by the end of this book, Barth and his theology emerge as *the* way forward for Christian thought, then Harnack can be safely forgotten. But if Barth's own views raise serious problems, then Harnack's criticisms cannot be brushed aside as easily as all that. We saw in the first chapter a prophecy made by Harnack, that Barth's way would open the floodgates for barbarianism and atheism, and we saw how Barth's theology was indeed followed by a situation of which this was an apt description, even though there were other outside forces involved in the process. For all the importance of Barth's stress on the Godness of God, had it necessarily to be put in quite that way? Even Barth, when he approached Harnack's age, grew more forbearing, and when he spoke to a group of ministers in 1956 in a hall in Aarau where he had had a furious encounter with Harnack a generation before, his topic was one which would have been impossible in these earlier days, 'The *Humanity* of God'.[18] Could this element, despite Barth's protests, not have been introduced much earlier to temper the starkness of *Romans*?

Perhaps not, at that stage. But in that case, how far can Harnack be faulted? We know Barth's position; to see it from Harnack's perspective, only a simple experiment is necessary. Let the reader take Harnack's brilliant lecture series, *What is Christianity*?, delivered in Berlin in 1899–1900, and read enough to get their flavour, or, if that is impracticable, let him listen to one short paragraph:

Unless all appearances are deceptive, no stormy crisis, no breach with his past, lies behind the period of Jesus' life that we know. In none of his sayings or discourses, whether he is threatening and punishing or drawing and calling people to him with kindness, whether he is speaking of his relation to the Father or to the world, can we discover the signs of inner revolutions overcome, or the scars of any terrible conflict. Everything seems to pour from him naturally, as though it could not do otherwise, like a spring from the depths of the earth, clear and unchecked in its flow. Where shall we find the man who at the age of thirty can so speak, if he has gone through bitter struggles – struggles of the soul, in which he has ended by burning what he once adored, and by adoring what he burned?[19]

Then let him compare what he has read with Barth's *Romans*, or the paragraph from it quoted in the previous chapter. Those without a theological training may well be surprised how much the Harnack of 1900 still speaks for them today, with his particular picture of Jesus and his stress on the brotherhood of man and the fatherhood of God. Those with theological training will have many criticisms to make, but like Rudolf Bultmann, who wrote the introduction to a recent reissue, they will still stand and admire, for Harnack's work was never less than impressive. If you had this perspective, a perspective which had grown on you over the years, would you have abandoned your heritage for the alternative that Barth had to offer?

Barth might be playing his own instrument, but at this time he was by no means alone. In addition to the faithful Thurneysen, who now published a full-length study of Dostoievsky, others had arrived by different routes at approximately the same point as Barth. 'God is other than the world, he is beyond the world, and this means the complete abrogation of the whole man, of his whole history.'[20] The words might have come from *Romans*, but in fact they were written by Rudolf Bultmann, whose early writings bear an uncanny resemblance to those of his contemporary. The year that Barth's second edition of *Romans* appeared, Friedrich Gogarten published a study entitled *The Religious Decision* and Emil Brunner a book entitled *Experience, Knowledge and Faith*. Although this concentration of publications was entirely fortuitous, it made the authors into a band of like-minded crusaders, and together they launched a journal to further their aims. After some discussion they decided to call it *Zwischen den Zeiten*, 'Between the Two Ages', taking up a phrase of Gogarten's which referred to the time of decision in which he believed that man was now standing. Its avowed aim was the development of a truly biblical theology, in line with the Reformers and in opposition to all liberal theology.

The collaboration lasted, in essentials, until 1933, the year of Hitler's rise to power, by which time the group behind it had begun to break up and go their different ways. From the beginning they had been a hastily-formed and somewhat disparate alliance, and as time went on it became clear that the tension between them was too great for the relationship to continue. By 1938, in a piece of autobiographical reminiscence, Barth was lamenting that all the others had departed from the road that he alone was following faithfully, and was dismissing his former friends in bitter terms, Gogarten as 'a sinister-looking German state theologian' and Brunner as a Buchmanite;[21] Bultmann had left the circle at a much earlier stage.

The aim of producing a theology that was truly biblical and in line with the Reformers was a pressing personal problem for Barth himself. He had made his negative contribution by blowing up the commonly held theological positions and destroying the ground on which they were built, but just as he could not lecture on Romans indefinitely, so he could not for ever leave unfilled the void left by his annihilation of existing systems. Yet what was to be put in its place that would meet his exacting requirements?

The answer to this question brings us to the turning point which led a man on whom had been laid the mantle of a prophet to devote himself to writing six million words of constructive exposition of his idea of the nature of the Christian faith. How this change was brought about is therefore of particular interest, and it is fortunate that Barth left sufficient indication of the process. It began in 1924, when Barth, who, amidst all this extra-curricular activity, still had his students to think about, decided to launch out on his own and teach a course of dogmatic theology. But how was he to set about it? He describes how he sat in his study in the spring vocation, mulling over the problem. His biblical and historical studies to date had more and more alienated him from virtually all theology of the present and of the recent past; he saw himself in the open, without a teacher. He was convinced that the Bible must be the controlling element in his work and that he

54

ought to link up with the Reformed tradition, but how was he to do it?

At that point he came across a recently republished volume of dogmatics by a nineteenth-century writer, Heinrich Heppe, now completely forgotten. It was out of date, dusty, unattractive, almost like a logarithm table, [dreary and apparently little more than the old orthodoxy. Yet Barth did not put it aside, and as he read more deeply, he found just what he wanted:

> I found myself visibly in the circle of the Church, and, moreover, in accordance with such prototypes, in the region of Church science, respectable of its kind. I had come to be amazed at the long, peaceful breathing, the sterling quality, the relevant strictness, the superior style, the methods confident at least themselves, with which this 'orthodoxy' had wrought. I had cause for astonishment at its wealth of problems and the sheer beauty of its trains of thought. In these old fellows I saw that it can be worth while to reflect upon the tiniest point with the greatest force of Christian presupposition, and, for the sake of much appealed-to 'life', to be quite serious about the question of truth all along the line. In other words I saw that Protestant dogmatics was once a careful, orderly business, and I conceived that it might perhaps become so again, if it could reacquire its obviously wandered nerves and return to a strict, churchly and scientific outlook.[22]

A good deal was to happen before Barth at last found himself on the right course, but that moment was without question the turning point, the time that changed the rest of Barth's life.

The nature of the course was decided, but before it could actually begin there was a small matter of university politics to be settled. Barth wanted to call his lectures 'Christian Dogmatics'. But in a Lutheran faculty Christian dogmatics were *de facto* Lutheran dogmatics, so Barth was asked to change the title to 'Reformed Dogmatics'. He refused, and appealed to higher authority, but lost his case, finally following Calvin in choosing the title 'Instruction in the Christian

Religion'.[23] This clash was just one of the many frustrations of Göttingen. From his third year onwards, Barth had been keeping his eyes open for other possibilities and had been weighing them up in his mind, but without any firm resolve. By the summer of the next year, 1925, however, it was clear that the time had come to move. The question was, where? Perhaps surprisingly, Barth seriously considered a return to parish life, despite the vast amount of work he had done to fit himself for professorial life. Barth's sense of scholarly inferiority still disturbed him. But there were considerations on the other side:

> I am troubled by the memory of how greatly, how yet more greatly, I failed finally as pastor of Safenwil. . . . The prospect of having to teach children again, of having to take hold of all kinds of practical problems is really fearful to me: simply because I feel that I cannot *do* it.[24]

Besides, something had been started among the students in Germany which was important for the future of theology in general. Was that to be abandoned? Thurneysen saw much to be said for a return to Switzerland, and other advisers told Barth that his place was in the pulpit. Barth was again in a dilemma. The principle 'against nature' was no help, because there were reasons for and against on both sides. He felt that he could be neither a proper professor nor a proper pastor.

> If only an angel would come and call to me through his trumpet (at least with a little plus sign!) that I am still fit for the one or the other! But I am afraid that I am really exactly in the balance. If I stood once more before the decision of 1921, I would *not* have the courage to become a professor, and neither have I now the courage to become a pastor.[25]

Almost in despair, Barth went to the state representative at the university and asked openly what his future in the system was likely to be. The answer was reassuring. Barth's work had not gone unnoticed. Germany did not want to lose him back to Switzerland, and there was a possibility of a move elsewhere. By July an offer had come through. Barth could move to a chair of Dogmatics and New Testament Exegesis at Münster.[26] The salary was attractive for a man with five children to educate and it was a full professorship. Barth generously made enquiries to see if Thurneysen could follow him to Göttingen, but it was not to be. The old story: not enough published work . . .[27]

With the move to Münster the period of uncertainty was over. Barth's future became clear. At this point the published correspondence with Thurneysen stops and we no longer have such detailed comment. But that is less important now. For with his continuing study, Barth was building up a range of learning that would soon remove for good and all any suggestion of inferiority of scholarship. He stayed at Münster until 1930 and then moved to Bonn. During this period he established the rest of his life's work and added to those who were to support him in it his closest companion of all. In 1929 Charlotte von Kirschbaum joined him as his secretary, to stand by Barth in his work and to share his home.

While Barth was a professor in Germany he wrote a good many articles and some more extended studies, but of his published works during the period only two are of comparable importance to *Romans* in illustrating the way in which his thought was progressing. These are his *Outline of Christian Dogmatics*, published from Münster in 1927, and his book on Anselm, *Fides Quaerens Intellectum*, which appeared shortly after his move to Bonn.

We left Barth grappling with the problem of how to lecture to his students on dogmatics and having just discovered a book which seemed to show him the way. The *Outline of*

Christian Dogmatics shows the consequences of his discovery put into practice. It is a further step in the desired direction, but still only a step. For *Christian Dogmatics* is an exact counterpart of the first edition of *Romans*. Once he sat down and read it through in print, Barth found himself wholly dissatisfied with what he had written, and set to work to fulfil his aims all over again. This time, however, the rewriting was to take much longer. It was not until 1932, after the help provided by his study of Anselm, that Barth really refined his method to his satisfaction, and though he could then see the way forward well enough, in the *Church Dogmatics* he never succeeded in reaching its end.

Christian Dogmatics begins with one of Barth's disarming prefaces, in which he explains what he is trying to do. First, he has to defend himself against the friends who will feel that he is letting the side down; can it be anything short of betrayal when a man who emerged as a fiery prophet eight years previously now writes, of all things, a volume of dogmatic theology?[28] Barth reminds his friends that he never wanted to be a prophet in the first place. It is in this context that he introduces the picture of the man stumbling up the church tower and grabbing the bell rope by mistake. That illustration is often quoted, but its sequel is usually left unnoticed. Barth in fact continues: 'The ringing of the bell is not what the man intended and he cannot and will not repeat the experience. On the contrary, having once seen what can happen he will continue his climb with the utmost possible caution.'[29] He insists that he was and is an ordinary theologian who has at his disposal not the word of God, but, at best, a doctrine of the word of God. He does not want to continue in the prophet's mantle with which others have endowed him. Nevertheless, there is something that has to be said now. He apologizes for writing at the beginning of his university career what wiser men usually leave for the end, but excuses himself by saying that it is better to speak inadequately to the present situation than to produce a respectable theology thirty years after the event.

Christian Dogmatics is a fascinating book, even if Barth did find it unsatisfactory, and it is a pity that it was never translated into English. Unfortunately, it is extremely difficult to summarize – as always, with Barth, the presentation is as important as the content – and it is impossible here to do more than ask what Barth set out to do and precisely why he decided that he had failed.

In *Romans*, it will be remembered, he had insisted that knowledge of God, and indeed faith itself, come directly from God without any achievement on man's side. In his systematic theology he was attempting to construct a more positive approach which did not betray his basic insight and which did not build any kind of way beginning on the human side, from man to God. His proposed solution is to begin with a leap straight into the situation that the Christian may be said to occupy. Without further ado, Barth takes his stand in the setting of the church and examines the contents of the knowledge of God that is actually possessed in the church: the doctrine of the Trinity, the doctrine of the person of Christ, the spirit, the word, faith, the church itself. His book is divided into four great chapters, dealing with the reality of the word of God as it comes to man, the revelation of God (Trinity, incarnation, spirit), scripture and preaching. Throughout the book the primacy of God is asserted again and again. In the church, in the scriptures, in the experience of the spirit, in the person of Jesus, in the word of preaching, God has spoken to man in such a way that man can hear him. This communication is in one direction and cannot be reversed: 'God is pure, indissoluble subject, even when he makes himself object in becoming flesh, scripture, preaching. He is and remains inaccessible to thought, or rather, he becomes accessible to thought in revelation only in all his accessibility, as the Master who cannot in any way be mastered by our thinking. Where he does become accessible, it is when his word speaks through the spirit and to the spirit, when the spirit speaks in the word and the spirit, the same spirit, hears in us.'[30]

Here was Barth's positive purpose put into practice, but the way in which it was carried out was still too near to the approach to be found in *Romans*, as can be detected even in the language of dialectic that Barth uses. The Word of God was still stressed as sheer act or eschatological event, the vertical from above, the tangent touching the circle. The miraculous character of the event was so heightened that there was no ground *within it* (which is what Barth insisted on looking for) on which to build a base for response. This meant that man's response had to come in outside the miracle of the divine intervention, involving Barth's theology in including some sort of existential decision. Consequently, the inclusion of such a human response in the essential nature of revelation in the end of the day meant some form of co-redemption.

This is the point that worried Barth more than anything else. Because of the way in which he had chosen to stress the transcendence of God, if he developed *Romans* into a more systematic pattern of thought he had to bring the decision of man to what was, for him, an impermissible degree. He found to his horror that he, who had been trying so long to escape from the approach typified by Schleiermacher, which began from man in order to get to God, had still not broken free. He read in his own work that the man who hears is bound up in the concept of the word of God as the God who speaks. Man is co-posited in this concept, like Schleiermacher's God in the 'feeling of absolute dependence'. Man, he had said, does not speak of the word of God unless in so doing he speaks of this word of God being perceived by man, or, still more concretely, of the man who perceives, the human 'I', which here ultimately and finally comes up against the Thou that is its origin and in community with which it can alone exist as I.[31] Shades of Martin Buber!

Three years later, Barth answered his problem satisfactorily in his book on Anselm, a study of the Archbishop of Canterbury's famous *Proslogion*, which has already been mentioned. His solution, despite the complex language in which it is put, is basically simple: he transfers the emphasis from God's action to his being, and bases the possibility of communication between God and man on the rationality of God. God is absolute wisdom, so his ways with man are also reasonable; that is not to say that we can construct them out of our own thoughts, but we can understand them and elucidate them after he has shown them to us. When we come to understand as believers, it is that the rationality of our believing mind has met up with the rationality of God, the object of our faith.

We are given faith by God, and the giving of faith is still a miracle, but as we are given faith, i.e. as God gives himself through his Word for us to know, we may be sure that it will be possible to move into clearer knowledge of what is given us to know by the use of our reason. Once this relationship between divine reason on the one hand and human reason on the other is established, then rational theology becomes possible, for all the miraculousness of its ultimate foundation.

To follow Barth's argument through, it is necessary to read his *Anselm* with some care. Much of it is very technical, but at the end Barth breaks out in a passage which foreshadows the best of his later theology, as well as being the rationale for it.

Anselm 'assumed' neither the Church's *Credo* nor his own *credere*, but he prayed and the Church's *Credo* and his own *credere* were assumed. God gave himself to him to know and he was able to know God. On this foundation, comparable to no philosophical presupposition and inconceivable for all systematic theology, he has come to know and has proved the Existence of God. For that reason his last word must be gratitude. Not satisfaction over a work that he has completed and that resounds to his own praise as its master, but gratitude for a work that has been done and of which he is in no sense the master.

God gave himself as the object of his knowledge and God illumined him that he might know him as object. Apart from this event there is no proof of the existence, that is of the reality, of God. But in the power of this event there is a proof which is worthy of gratitude. It is truth that has spoken and not man in search of faith. Man might not want faith. Man might remain always a fool. As we heard, it is of grace if he does not. But even if he did, 'if I did not wish to know Thee', truth has spoken – in such a way that cannot be ignored, refuted or forgotten and in such a way that man is forbidden and to that extent is unable not to recognize it. Just because it is the science of faith about faith, theology possesses light, but it is not the light of the theologian's faith.[32]

After *Anselm*, the place of dialectic in Barth's theology is taken by analogy. The relationship between God and man that makes theology possible is an analogical one. 'Analogy,' says the *Shorter Oxford English Dictionary*, is 'a resemblance of relations or attributes as a ground of reasoning.' But here we have to tread carefully. What kind of an analogy? All his life Barth had a horror of the kind of analogy that suggested that there was something in the being of man that had its parallel in the being of God. He felt that Roman Catholic theology was based on a presupposition of this kind (and in so doing showed insufficient understanding); for him, analogy must be an analogy of *faith*. Now faith, as we have seen, is something given by God, so this analogy has its starting place in God. We do not understand God by analogies from our own experience, but understand ourselves by analogy from God. One of Barth's commentators has explained this idea brilliantly by the illustration of an hour-glass or egg-timer. The sand in the hour-glass moves only from above to below, and not vice versa; as it trickles through the narrow passage in the centre and falls to the bottom, it begins a move in the opposite direction, from below upwards: thus the two halves are related, for the top makes its impression on the bottom – but everything depends on the top.[33]

To continue the illustration, the narrow passage in the centre through which the sand must trickle is, for Barth, the person of Jesus Christ. In his earlier work, God and man were set in stark contrast; now they are separated and at the same time united through the mediation of Jesus Christ. He is the channel through which everything happens. From now on Barth's theology is to be uncompromisingly Christocentric. God is to be found only in Jesus Christ – and Jesus Christ is to be found only in and through the scripture that witnesses to him.

Barth's use of Anselm makes more urgent a question that was already raised by his use of Paul in *Romans*: how much of Barth's interpretation of Anselm is Anselm himself, and how much of it is Barth? Just what kind of interpretation is it that Barth is employing? Would Anselm understand himself from Barth's picture? Would Paul? The question is the most serious that can be put to Barth, because interpretation of other writers, interpretation of scripture, is the dominant feature of his theology. What principles does he adopt? On what basis does he engage in his rational response to the God who offers himself to be known? On what basis does he rethink the thoughts of other men?

More conventional scholars would question Barth's

interpretations of both Paul and Anselm. By their standards they would regard his work as eccentric and highly individualistic. There can be no doubting his personal, creative brilliance, but by the usual criteria it seems lacking in objective control. The same criticism could be made of Barth's fascinating survey of Protestant theology in the nineteenth century, part of which has been translated into English under the title *From Rousseau to Ritschl*. As a one-man interpretation it is a *tour de force*, but one cannot help wondering whether it is any fairer a picture of those it portrays than was Lytton Strachey's *Eminent Victorians*, albeit slanted in a rather different direction.

Barth was happiest arguing with those who were no longer in a position to reply in person. His regular inability to see particular points made by an opponent often makes the controversies in which he is engaged rather painful reading. For all his revisions and abandonments of his own works, he obviously found it very difficult indeed to confess *to anyone else* that they were right and he was wrong. And of course anyone as single-minded as Barth is extremely difficult to shift off course.

The most famous argument in which Barth ever engaged illustrates all this well. It was carried on in 1934, in written form, between Barth and his former friend Emil Brunner, over the question of natural theology, that is, whether any natural revelation of God may be said to be found in creation outside Jesus Christ. The English translation, published in 1946 under the title *Natural Theology*, just about conveys the vigorous language which make the controversy a classic of polemics. Brunner manages to retain his good humour longer than Barth, but at times there is little to choose.

Attacking Barth straight away for his one-sidedness, Brunner compares him to a loyal soldier on sentry duty at night, who shoots everyone who does not give the password as he has been commanded and who therefore from time to time annihilates a good friend whose password he does not hear or misunderstands in his eagerness.[34] Barth confirms the description by retorting: 'You do not stare at the serpent, with the result that it stares back at you, hypnotizes you, and is ultimately certain to bite you, but you hit it and kill it as soon as you see it.'[35] Brunner's point is that the centre of theological concern has shifted; fifteen years ago the themes were dictated by liberal theology and the question of 'religion'; now, however, that battle has been won, and the supreme importance of the Word of God is recognized. But how exclusive is this Word? Is it necessary to maintain unflinchingly, as does Barth, that there is no point of contact for the word of God in man, that there is complete discontinuity between grace and creation? Is not Barth going contrary to the Bible and proving more Reformed than the Reformers? Furthermore, is he not putting unnecessary barriers in front of simpler people (remember Harnack's accusation?): to neglect the question of natural theology, man's own capacity, is to neglect pastoral care: 'What I should say to a man upon his death-bed is a holy matter; but it is a matter no less holy how I am to say it to him in such a way that he shall understand and appreciate it. A pastor might – to put it somewhat strongly – go to heaven on account of the What but go to hell on account of the How ... The What is, as it were, guarded by faith, but the How has to be guarded by love.'[36] Does Barth take love seriously enough?

In his reply Barth stands by the position which we have already seen him attain. He manages to find justifiable fault in Brunner's argument and may be said to demolish Brunner's alternative position. He does not, however, give a satisfactory answer to Brunner's criticisms of his own.

He castigates Brunner unmercifully for bringing to birth a new and great danger, even rejecting Brunner's remarks about pastoral care. Barth's own experience is that people are reached best when he relies least on there being anything in which he can awaken an echo, when he allows what he says to be dictated by the subject matter. He is just not interested in the methodology of preaching; he is just not interested in what people may or may not understand; he is just not interested in what Brunner is saying. In short, in the one-word title of his reply, his answer is 'No!'.

Even Barth's greatest admirers would find it hard to defend everything in this piece, as they would find it hard to defend his later attack on Bultmann. But here they can remind us of one extenuating factor. This argument was being carried on in Germany in 1934, with Hitler in power, when far more was at stake than merely a matter of theological principle.

NOTES

1. *RTM*, p. 74.
2. *RTM*, pp. 76f.
3. *RTM*, p. 93.
4. *RTM*, p. 79.
5. *RTM*, pp. 143, 160.
6. *RTM*, p. 101.
7. *RTM*, p. 104.
8. *RTM*, p. 76.
9. *RTM*, p. 106.
10. *RTM*, p. 80.
11. Agnes von Zahn-Harnack, *Adolf von Harnack*, pp. 531ff.
12. *Adolf von Harnack*, p. 535.
13. *RTM*, p. 79.
14. *RTM*, pp. 49f., see pp. 127f., 144.
15. *Adolf von Harnack*, p. 535.
16. *Adolf von Harnack*, p. 534.
17. Quoted in Heinz Zahrnt, *The Question of God*, Collins 1969, p. 41.
18. Karl Barth, *The Humanity of God*, Fontana Books 1967, pp. 33–64.
19. Adolf von Harnack, *What is Christianity?*, Harper Torchbooks 1957, pp. 33f.
20. Rudolf Bultmann, *Faith and Understanding*, SCM Press 1969, p. 40.
21. *HCM*, pp. 41f.

22. Foreword to H. Heppe, *Reformed Dogmatics*, Allen & Unwin 1950, pp. vf.

23. *RTM*, pp. 166f., 181ff.   24. *RTM*, p. 230.

25. *RTM*, p. 231.   26. *RTM*, p. 232.

27. *RTM*, p. 236.   28. *Christliche Dogmatik*, p. viii.

29. *Christliche Dogmatik*, p. ix.

30. *Christliche Dogmatik*, pp. 454f.

31. *Christliche Dogmatik*, p. 111.

32. *Anselm*, pp. 170f.

33. H. U. von Balthasar, *Karl Barth. Eine Darstellung und Deutung seiner Theologie*, Verlag Jakob Hegner, Köln 1961, p. 210.

34. Karl Barth and Emil Brunner, *Natural Theology*, Geoffrey Bles 1947, p. 16.

35. *Natural Theology*, p. 76.   36. *Natural Theology*, p. 58.

4 Politician

So far we have considered Barth as a thinker. During the 1930s, however, his thought had far-reaching political consequences and was a matter not only of theory, but of practice. This is not an unexpected development, for Barth had always been interested in politics, and indeed had been involved in them in his early days. So when Hitler's policies began to take effect, Barth was not venturing on to new ground for the first time.

Barth's friend Thurneysen interested him in the work of Christoph Blumhardt, a remarkable German pastor with an equally remarkable father, Johann, who between 1900 and 1906 had occupied a seat as a member of the Socialist party in the state legislature of Württemberg, an unheard-of thing for an ordained minister to do. Together they actually went to see Blumhardt at Bad Boll, the retreat centre that his father had founded, and the same year Barth joined the Social Democrats. But he did so with hesitation. He had rooted objections to the identification of the kingdom of God with social questions, and felt it to be a danger to the gospel. On the other side, less theologically-minded members of the party found his particular emphasis a bit too much to take. There is a story of Barth addressing a meeting and then being accosted by a Social Democrat afterwards; the man granted that Barth seemed to have spoken the mind of Jesus – but wasn't there something rather easier for them to do?[1]

The man who in his first year as a professor warned his friends not to waste time reading the paper was an avid reader himself. At Safenwil his purpose was 'to have the Bible in one hand and the newspaper in the other', but this proved more difficult than he expected: 'One broods alternately over the newspaper and the New Testament and actually sees fearfully little of the organic connection between the two worlds concerning which one should now be able to give a clear and powerful witness. Or is it different with you?'[2] During the 1920s this particular preoccupation faded into the background; Barth's theme, to be repeated several times in later years as Europe was involved in cataclysm after cataclysm, was that it was his vocation to carry on theology, and only theology, as if nothing had happened.[3] However, outside pressure grew on him to make some comment on the politics of the Third Reich, and eventually he yielded and responded in characteristic fashion. It is interesting to note how and when he chose his moment.

The success of National Socialism and the election of Adolf Hitler as Chancellor of Germany was by no means unwelcome to the churches. The corruption and decadence brought about by the economic and social collapse of the 'twenties had scandalized church leaders of all traditions, who now found much to approve of in a movement which emphasized patriotism, discipline, unity, sacrifice – and protection against the menace of communism. For his part, Hitler had subordinated personal dislike of Christianity to tactical deceit, and used the churches to help him on his way. Although official church policy remained neutral, Catholics went over to Nazism in large numbers, and after the assurance of fair and generous treatment for the churches in Hitler's Reichstag speech of March 1933, it was only four months before a truce was signed between Hitler and the

Vatican. Leaders of the Protestant churches were even willing to work out a theological backing for Nazi ideals, but in the long run their views were much more disparate, and they proved the only Christians to put up any sort of a fight.[4]

From the 1920s onwards, groups of German Protestant pastors, who tended on the whole to be politically conservative, patriotic and paternalistic, had been banding themselves into associations aimed at giving a purely German character to the Christian gospel. 'For a German,' one of the milder statements goes, 'the Church is the community of believers who are obligated to fight for a Christian Germany.'[5] Another statement indicates on which of the last two words the accent is to be put: 'A godless fellow-countryman is nearer to us than one of another race, even if he sings the same hymn or prays the same prayer.'[6] To begin with, these German Christian groups were as scattered and separate as the German churches themselves, but in 1933 a movement for a single national church with a bishop at its head gained increasing momentum, with the full approval of Hitler, who foresaw that such a church would be easier to control in the Nazi interest. Hitler chose his National Bishop, a mediocre Nazi named Ludwig Müller, who was given the task of engineering his own election as soon as possible. However, other groups in the church, organized by men like Walter Künneth, Martin Niemöller and the young Dietrich Bonhoeffer, offered considerable resistance, and succeeded in electing Friedrich von Bodelschwingh, director of a large church hospital and welfare centre in Westphalia. The German Christians at once launched a vigorous campaign demanding the reversal of the election and the institution of Müller; less than a month later, the Prussian Minister of Education had appointed a commissar for the church who raided offices and suspended senior ministers; in despair, Bodelschwingh had to resign.

At this point Barth joined the battle with a fifteen thousand word pamphlet, written over a weekend, entitled *Theological Existence Today*.[7] The title indicates the theme: existence today must be theological. In other words, the one and all-important thing for Christians is the word of God. Barth relates this theme to three current issues. First, the demand on all sides for church reform. Reform can be carried out by the church only on the basis of the word. There can be no second, alternative standard, say, social and political conditions. Secondly, the election of a bishop. But what kind of a bishop?, Barth asks. There seem only two likely models, the Roman Catholic prelacy, and the Leadership of Adolf Hitler. Both are unthinkable; there is one leader and one leader alone, Jesus Christ. Finally, he comes to the question of the German Christians. Why has he said nothing so far? Because until now he had thought that the answer to be given to the German Christians was obvious, and others had been giving it clearly. But now some of his own friends have joined the German Christian movement. So he must make it plain once and for all that the answer is NO! The church preaches the gospel in the state, but not under it and in its spirit. He ends with a call for a spiritual centre of resistance. Theological existence is not an end in itself; it serves the nation, but does so in sole obedience to the word.

As Barth remarked, looking back on the immediate results of his statement, he was saying nothing new. We, too, can recognize the familiar emphasis and exclusiveness. But now what he had to say had no vestige of an academic theory. It became a challenge, a political force. Barth had not changed, but circumstances had.[8]

Various groups of Protestant ministers working against the German Christians now rapidly moved towards the formation of a church confessedly built on the word of God and the Reformed credal statements, in opposition to 'German' Christianity, to be known in the future as the 'Confessing Church'. It came into being as a result of two synods held at Barmen, one of the two towns making up the huge industrial centre of Wuppertal. At the second of these synods, Barth, 'while the others were taking their afternoon nap', drafted a declaration which was to be the charter of the new church. Its first article indicates its tone:

In view of the destructive errors of the German Christians and the present national church government, we pledge ourselves to the following evangelical truths:

1. 'I am the way and the truth and the life: no man comes to the Father but by me' (John 14.6).
'Truly, truly, I say to you, he who does not enter by the door into the sheepfold but climbs up some other way is a thief and a robber . . . I am the door: by me if any man enter in, he shall be saved' (John 10.1, 9).

Jesus Christ, as he is testified to us in Holy Scripture, is the one Word of God which we are to hear, which we are to trust and obey in life and in death.
We repudiate the false teaching that the Church can and must recognize yet other happenings and powers, personalities and truths, as divine revelation alongside this one Word of God, as a source of her preaching.[9]

Here is not the place to continue the story of the Confessing Church; it has been told in detail elsewhere. But Barth's contribution to it and inspiration of it cannot be emphasized too much. Something of the magnetism that he exercised can be seen in the correspondence that was carried on at this time between him and Dietrich Bonhoeffer, who later was to prove the church's most distinguished member. But Barth's personal involvement in the affairs of the German church was soon to cease. As professor of theology in Bonn he was employed by the state (he had been obliged to become a German citizen on his move to Münster), and therefore had to take an oath of allegiance to Hitler. He refused, and in December 1934, six months after the second Barmen synod, he was suspended. He appealed to a tribunal and in June 1935 was declared not guilty. The Minister of Education reversed the verdict and Barth had to leave the country; had it not been for the Swiss citizenship that he still retained, doubtless things would have gone much worse for him. Three days after his dismissal, the Basel City Council elected him to the university chair in theology there.[10]

Between 1929 and the outbreak of the Second World War, Barth's horizons began to be widened in other ways. Hitherto, he had left Switzerland and Germany only to visit Holland, but in the next decade he went to Italy, to enjoy classical antiquity, to Denmark, France, Austria, Czechoslovakia, Hungary and Transylvania. 'I do not know,' he wrote in 1938, 'how it ever came about that there was a time when I could exist without having been spoken to, more or less distinctly, by all those distant places, by their history, and by the present state of their people.'[11] He discovered the detective story and became a 'very bad but very passionate horseman'. He felt that he had never lived more gaily in the everyday world than in this period, in which others thought that his theology had taken on a monkish concentration. Rather than falling into an abstract negation of the world, he had become simultaneously very much more churchly and very much more worldly.

That may be so, but these comments of Barth's, coming as they do after an account of his stand on the German church question, cannot be allowed to pass without one critical comment. In 1937 and 1938 Barth also travelled to Great Britain, primarily to give the Gifford Lectures (in a way that would have made their founder turn in his grave, as they were instituted as a defence of natural theology!); during his second visit he stayed in Oxford and lectured at

Lady Margaret Hall on *The Trouble and Promise of the Church Struggle in Germany*.[12] His message is in the same terms as *Theological Existence* of 1933. There is no freedom for the church in Germany; it is being systematically corrupted and suppressed; in the face of this persecution the Confessing Church has discovered the 'majesty of the Word of God, as the bread on which she may nourish herself, as the fountain from which she may drink'. But towards the end of the lecture Barth asks another question: 'Why, one hears it asked, have the Christians in Germany not been able to prevent the horrors of National Socialism, the concentration camps, the persecutions of the Jews? Still more: where were the Christians in Germany when this National Socialism first arose?'[13]

He reminds his audience that the situation in Germany has been more complicated than they could imagine, that the beginnings of the Hitler movement were not easy to recognize. At least a small proof of faith has been given, and could the Christians in any country do better? All this may be true; and it might be added that a recent study of the Nazi persecution of the churches has shown how hopeless any resistance to Hitler was in the long run. Certainly, the knife edge provided by Barth's theology seems to have been the only weapon sharp enough to cut through the web of lies, fantasies and perversions constructed by the German Christians. Nevertheless, what is to be said of a theology which says nothing of the downright and utter evil of the Nazi policy of violence, torture and genocide in purely human, this-worldly ethical terms, which is silent on the massacre of the Jews and the corruption of national life as evils *per se*? Here is the price that an approach like that which Barth began with *Romans* has to pay. One longs for him to say, just once, 'In the name of mankind, this is wicked', for him to show some insight into what other men, women and children think and feel and suffer as fellow human beings. But this he cannot do. Is the concentration on the Word, on Jesus Christ and him alone, worth this neglect? Whatever benefits Barth's championing of the Confessing Church brought, it was bound up with some terrible connotations from which he never managed to escape.

Barth continued his support for the German Confessing Church from Switzerland. The place of *Zwischen den Zeiten*, the journal from which Barth had parted in 1933, was taken by a series entitled *Theological Existence Today*, named after Barth's first intervention; these short monographs were eagerly awaited by pastors who looked to them for guidance. A stream of other communications flowed out of Switzerland in support of the church, and as the war closed in, Barth wrote a series of open letters to the European countries under attack from Germany. To the Czechs, in the person of Dr Hromadka in Prague, he wrote in 1938 that not only the freedom of Europe but that of the church had to be defended on the frontier of Bohemia; he also wrote to the French Protestants in 1939/40, to the Norwegians, Dutch and Americans in 1942 and, in 1941, to the English, at the invitation of A. R. Vidler and J. H. Oldham.[14] Writing at Easter, he takes as a text the saying of the risen Jesus 'All power is given to me in heaven and in earth', arguing that it is essential for his readers to trust in Jesus Christ alone rather than 'natural law', his term for the English attitude which, he felt, prevented people from seeing what had been happening theologically in the church in Germany. The underlying argument is familiar, yet the letter also seems to contain one discordant note to which we must return later: Barth argues that when the British Government declared war in 1939 it acted as the government of a righteous state according to Christian standards; at the same time, this was true of Switzerland when she resolved, at the same time, on the armed defence of her neutrality, the maintenance of which is her historic mission. How is that position reached on Barth's theological premises?

Barth's contribution was not limited to words. He joined the Society for Aid to the Confessing Church in Germany, and was among those helping Pastor Paul Vogt in his work of caring for foreign, and especially Jewish, refugees. He joined a secret organization for the defence of Switzerland in case of invasion, and in 1940 actually took his place in the ranks of Sentry Company 5, a military unit involved in keeping a lookout along the Swiss frontiers. He welcomed this experience as he looked back on it: 'As never before, it brought me intimately face to face with the common men of my country, with whom I lived day and night.' He preached to them from time to time, and 'learned anew how a sermon really aimed at a man must be constructed'.[15]

As the war at last seemed to be coming to an end, he travelled vigorously round Switzerland delivering lectures on the nature of the policy which he believed ought to be adopted towards defeated Germany, lectures which were published the same year as a pamphlet entitled *The Germans and Ourselves*.[16] We do not know enough about the German people, he argues, or what historical forces have shaped their nation. They are victims of a development which goes back as far as Frederick the Great. But that past has been destroyed with the war; Germany cannot be the same. They must therefore be given a chance to start afresh. This is the message of the gospel. 'Come unto me, you unlikeable ones, you wicked Hitler boys and girls, you brutal S.S. soldiers, you evil Gestapo police, you sad compromisers and collaborationists, all you men of the herd who have moved so long in patient stupidity behind your so-called leader. Come unto me, and I will refresh you; I will start afresh from zero with you.'[17] This is the gospel, and as the Swiss listen to it they must not forget that they, too, have their sins, and are not free of the peril of self-righteousness.

His words made him unpopular with Germans and Swiss alike: with the Germans, because they objected to his analysis of their history; with the Swiss because no one likes to be told home truths. But the document is almost Barth's best piece of political writing, permeated with a balanced mixture of Christian teaching and insight into the human situation which he did not always achieve.

Again, words were matched by actions. During the spring and summer of 1945, Barth made contact with the Movement for a Free Germany, where for the first time he came to know prominent Communists and, he adds, their methods. American help enabled him to return to Germany in the autumn to assist in the re-formation of the Council of Brethren of the Confessing Church and in the organization of the official German Protestant Church. From this point on, however, the focal point of political interest was to shift from defeated Nazism to the growing influence of Communism. Here Barth's reactions were as eagerly expected as they had been a decade or more earlier.

Barth's comments on Communism were first made in the context of a visit to Hungary in 1948. He gave everyone a surprise. Far from comparing Communism to the earlier menace of Nazism, he refused to talk of the two movements in similar terms. In his view the situations of the 1930s and the late 1940s were quite different, and the position of the church in Hungary had to be judged 'quite independently from the point of view of the gospel and past developments'.[18] There were more important things to do than to attack Communism.

In Budapest, he was asked: 'What should the Christian

attitude be to a state that pays no attention to justice, which may be a godless state, which nevertheless pretends to be a friend of the church, but which must turn out sooner or later to be an enemy of the church, for inescapable ideological reasons? What should the church's attitude be to a state which allows the church to carry on independently for the time being, for purely tactical reasons, but also intimates that it will fight the church in the future?'[19]

Barth's reply is uncharacteristically hesitant. We shall not meet a perfect Christian state, he says, until the day of judgment, nor the devil's state either. We shall always be moving between the two. So even if the state seems to be showing signs of the beast from the abyss, we shall not immediately confront ourselves with the alternatives, Yes or No? Consent or martyrdom? Just because we are Christians we shall be free to wait a little and give ourselves time to examine the whole situation in detail.

> I am afraid that these questions betray the uneasiness of a mistrust that is not Christian. What I should like to do, therefore, would be to put my hand on the shoulders of those who have sent in these questions and ask: 'Ferryman, tell me honestly: is the situation really as dangerous as all that?' (quotation from a popular song). Already so dangerous today? It might become more dangerous – I know the way these things work out. But does it not still hold good that we should not fret over tomorrow, even though there may be good cause to ask anxiously: What will they do tomorrow? What has the Christian church to fear if it has faith? What can the kind of state adumbrated in these questions do to it?[20]

When his position became known in the West, it was viewed with incredulity, amazement and hostility, particularly in West Germany. Barth's old sparring partner Emil Brunner wrote an open letter in the same year, summing up his own problems about Barth's attitude. Why is Barth so equivocal now when he was so clear-cut in the 'thirties? Granted there are differences, but are not both Nazism and Communism forms of totalitarianism? Will Barth agree that a decided No is to be said by the Christian church to totalitarianism of any kind? It worries Brunner that even at the height of Barth's struggle against Nazism, he always avoided this question. He would never say that the totalitarian state is *eo ipso* an unjust, inhuman and godless state. And Brunner goes on at length to elaborate particular difficulties that he has over the line Barth follows.

Barth retorts that Brunner does not understand. Barth himself does not like Communism, and anyone who wants from him a political disclaimer of the system can have it at once. But what is given cheaply can be had cheaply. The situation is very different from 1933. It is not the duty of Christians, or of the church, to give theological backing to what every citizen can, with much shaking of his head, read in his daily paper, and what is so admirably expressed by Mr Truman and the Pope. No, when the church witnesses, it moves in fear and trembling, not with the stream but against it. And if an emergency does come, the church will profit more from the first article of Barmen than from knowledge of the objectionableness of totalitarianism.[21]

Barth was not completely neutral towards the situation in Communist countries over the next decade. In March 1953, he protested to Herr Zaisser, Minister of State in East Germany, about the arrest of pastors there during a persecution which lasted from February to July of that year. But then in 1956, the year of the Russian invasion of Hungary, he had nothing to say. The American theologian Reinhold Niebuhr attacked him bitterly in an article entitled 'Why doesn't Karl Barth speak about Hungary?', accusing him of impartiality at the price of moral irrelevance, but Barth would not be drawn. He kept silent until August 1958, when in a published 'Letter to a Pastor in the German Democratic Republic' he began by taking up Niebuhr's question.[22]

This question, he remarked, was asked from the secure stronghold of a hard-boiled Western politician, who wanted to lead his opponent on to thin ice either to provoke an anti-Communist statement or to put him in the position of being a crypto-Communist. Only when a question came to him actually out of the situation, in the form of a letter from a pastor in East Germany, did he feel that it was appropriate to express himself in print. Even then, he was hesitant, because inevitably he did not have first-hand knowledge of the situation.

He prefaces his advice with a reminder of I Peter 5.9: 'Because your adversary the devil, as a roaring lion, walks about looking for someone to devour.' Who, he asks, is this adversary? Is it Communism? Before the identification is made, it is worth looking rather more closely. There are ways in which Communism can take the form of the adversary, but so, too, can Western society – and he recalls how, in the sixteenth century, thinking of the Turks and the Pope, Protestant Christians talked of the Eastern and the Western Antichrist. Might it not be the same now?

The key, now as ever, is to love Jesus and him only in the situation, joyfully and gladly. Barth can even delight in the impossibility of giving public expressions of Christianity in Communist countries, in the absence of organizations and their influence, because this highlights what for him is the real nature of Christianity. While he is unwilling to take over the phrase 'the end of the Constantinian era' (he does not like thinking in these terms), he accepts what it stands for.

Barth's correspondent had raised some practical questions about the day-to-day conditions of life in East Germany, obviously having conditions in the Third Reich at the back of his mind. What about the required declaration of loyalty to the state, which Barth refused to give in Germany?

What does the declaration say?, asks Barth; it makes all the difference whether it is clear in its requirements or whether it is asking, as Hitler did, for a 'cat in the bag'. Loyalty to the order means fitting in with it. It does not mean accepting the ideology underlying the order. It includes the provision of freedom of thought over against the ideology, even to the point of conflict and revolt. What about the restrictions on the public proclamation of the gospel by the church?, asks the correspondent. Barth retorts that the church has no 'claim' on being able to preach the word publicly. What is required is service, and this becomes public only when God so wills. Restriction of the public proclamation of the church can even be God's work of love.

That same year, Barth summed up his thoughts on the 'East–West problem', as he insisted on calling it, in the third of a series of articles that he contributed to *The Christian Century* at ten-yearly intervals on 'How I changed my mind'. The degree to which the issue had been exercising Barth is indicated by the fact that no less than half the article is exclusively devoted to it.

Barth asserts that he believes anti-Communism as a matter of principle to be an evil even greater than Communism itself. Communism is a natural result of Western developments, and the total, inhuman compulsion of which the West complains has haunted the allegedly free world for centuries. Furthermore, the 'absolute enemy' relationship, to which so many in the West seem committed, is a heritage of past dictatorships: only the 'Hitler in us' can be an anti-Communist on principle. The West has failed to think through the situation that has developed since 1945 with Eastern eyes. Was not Russia provoked by the formation of NATO and West German rearmament, not to mention nuclear weapons:

Moreover, what kind of Western philosophy and political ethics – and unfortunately even theology – was it whose wisdom consisted in recasting the Eastern collective man into an angel of darkness and the Western 'organization man' into an angel of light? And then with the help of such metaphysics and mythology (the fact of an Eastern counterpart is no excuse!) bestowing on the absurd 'cold war' struggle its needed higher consecration? Were we so unsure of the goodness of the Western cause and of the power of resistance of Western man that we could bring ourselves to admit only senselessly unequal alternatives – freedom and the dignity of man as against mutual atomic annihilation – then venture to pass off just this latter alternative as a work of true Christian love?[23]

Because of his own point of view, Barth continues, people have represented him – when they did not label him directly a crypto-Communist or fellow traveller – either as a politically naive dilettante or, in a disapproving comparison with some Old Testament prophets, as a nonconformist in principle who gets a mischievous pleasure out of confounding the bourgeoisie. Above all, he has been the subject of attacks in Germany (both East and West!) and his native Switzerland. He already anticipates reading the necrology in which he is said to have done valuable service to the renewal of theology and in the German church struggle, but also to have been a political will-o'-the-wisp.

What are we to make of Barth's political thought? Are we to pass on him the judgment that he expected? That would not be impossible, but rather than attempting to judge, it might be more profitable to attempt to understand something of the influences underlying his political thought.

Some of the explanation of Barth's later political views may lie in his early sympathies. We have seen that he began as a Socialist, under the influence of Christian Socialists. It is here that his basic objections to the capitalist system have their origin. But Barth did not remain a *Christian* Socialist; as we noticed at the beginning of the chapter, with the second edition of *Romans* he had abandoned the connection between Christianity and Socialism. Now he was more thoroughgoing a revolutionary against the existing order than the most extreme Marxist, for society expresses the primal rebellion of man against God. In his views here, Barth has been compared not only with Karl Marx, but with Nietzsche and even the Anabaptists.[24]

Strangely enough, Barth seems to have very little direct acquaintance with Communism or Communist writing. This lack of familiarity extends even to the works of Marx himself. One commentator remarked of Barth's relationship to Marx that he seems to have been 'a cousin who did not know him, so to speak, but who shared the same spiritual ancestors, and the same revolutionary drive against the pretensions and complacency of bourgeois society'.[25] It seems harsh to criticize one who read so widely for not reading widely enough, but Barth's failure to familiarize himself with the kind of thinking about socialist Christianity that had been going on in his lifetime leads him to miss opportunities and perpetuate misunderstandings. Barth, regrettably, thought out his ethics in this area in a vacuum, or at best with the help of a group of congenial writers. The miracle is that the result comes out as well as it does.

Certainly it is hard to link Barth's many sober judgments on moral, political and economic questions directly with the theoretical theological basis which he outlined in two short works. One of these works appeared immediately before the Second World War and the other immediately after it: the first was entitled *Justification and Justice* (published in English as *Church and State*),[26] the second *The Christian Community and the Civil Community*.[27] Those who wish to pursue Barth's thinking further in this direction should see what he has to say at first hand; here there is room only for one comment on Barth's method.

His theology is, as always now, centred on Christ and the

Bible, and it proceeds by biblical exposition and analogy, following the line first discovered with *Anselm*. What is disturbing when such an approach is applied to political thinking is the apparent lack of control on the exposition itself and the formation of analogies. Even the starting points seem arbitrary in the extreme, as when for example at the beginning of *Church and State* the encounter between Pilate and Jesus is used as a parable for church–state relations. Is this, one might ask, because the New Testament is rather short of possible starting points and can offer nothing better?

The problem becomes acuter with the line of argument in *The Christian Community and the Civil Community*. Here the principle of analogy is played for all it is worth. The grace of God, revealed from heaven, shines on the church on earth, and is reflected from the church to the earthly state, the relationship between the three being one of analogy. Barth summarizes the aspects of this analogy in a series of principles. The church is based on the knowledge of the one eternal God who as such became man; therefore in the political sphere the church will always and in all circumstances be interested primarily in human beings and not in some abstract cause or other. The church is witness of the divine justification; therefore the church will be found where all political activity is in all circumstances regulated by a commonly acknowledged law. The church is witness that the Son of man came to seek and save the lost; therefore the church must concentrate first on the lower and lowest levels of society. The church is the fellowship of those who are freely called by the word of grace; therefore every citizen must be guaranteed the freedom to carry out his decisions in the politically lawful sphere. As the fellowship of those who live in one faith under one Lord on the basis of a baptism in one spirit, the church will stand for the

84

equality and freedom of all. The church lives from the disclosure of the true God in the light of Jesus Christ; therefore the church is the sworn enemy of all secret policies and secret diplomacy. And so he continues.[28]

The trouble is, as can easily be seen, that the analogies Barth chooses to draw are by no means the only possible ones. A German theologian with views not too dissimilar to those of Barth on theological questions pointed out, not unjustly, that while Barth argues from the disclosure of God in Christ that the church must be opposed to secret diplomacy, from the 'Messianic secret' in the gospels one could come to exactly the opposite conclusion. Similarly, the argument from 'one Lord, one faith, one baptism' could end up in the Nazi slogan 'One people, one nation, one leader'.[29] The criticism is perhaps a cheap one, but it cannot be ignored. By concentrating the focal point of his theology in God rather than in man, Barth runs the risk, as we have seen, of ignoring the human situation in all its complexity. He falls into the habit, of which the church is so often accused, of passing judgment before he is in full possession of the facts.

In any case, is Barth's chosen principle one that he can maintain consistently? We have already seen that Barth's practice of constructing analogies suffers from a lack of control and inadequate criteria. But some criteria are there – for instance Barth's tendency always to arrive at some form of democracy. Is it Barth's system that provides the criteria and controls, or do they slip in unnoticed, from elsewhere? If, as seems likely, the latter is the case, we have not only the insidious problem of hidden presuppositions; we also have to ask the crucial question whether Barth's theology is consistently usable in the political sphere.

NOTES

1. *RTM*, p. 27.
2. *RTM*, p. 45.
3. E.g. *HCM*, p. 52.
4. For a survey of church resistance to Hitler, see J. S. Conway, *The Nazi Persecution of the Churches 1933–45*, Weidenfeld & Nicolson 1968, esp. chs. 1–3.
5. Conway, p. 31.
6. Dietrich Bonhoeffer, *No Rusty Swords*, p. 210.
7. An English translation was published by Hodder & Stoughton in 1933.
8. *HCM*, p. 46.
9. The full text is quoted in E. H. Robertson, *Christians against Hitler*, SCM Press 1962, pp. 48–52.
10. A. B. Come, *An Introduction to Barth's Dogmatics for Preachers*, SCM Press 1963, pp. 53f.
11. *HCM*, pp. 39f.
12. Published by The Clarendon Press, 1938.
13. *Trouble and Promise*, p. 24.
14. Karl Barth, *A Letter to Great Britain from Switzerland*, The Sheldon Press 1941. An appendix includes the two letters to the French Protestants.
15. *HCM*, p. 53.
16. Karl Barth, *The Germans and Ourselves*, James Nisbet 1945.
17. *The Germans and Ourselves*, p. 40.
18. *HCM*, p. 57.
19. *Against the Stream*, p. 97.
20. *Against the Stream*, p. 98.
21. *Against the Stream*, pp. 106–124.
22. Karl Barth (with Johannes Hamel), *How to Serve God in a Marxist Land*, Association Press, New York 1959.
23. *HCM*, p. 64.
24. Charles West, *Communism and the Theologians*, SCM Press 1958, p. 181.
25. *Communism and the Theologians*, pp. 188f.
26. SCM Press 1939.
27. Included in *Against the Stream*, pp. 13–50.
28. *Against the Stream*, pp. 34–42.
29. Helmut Thielicke, quoted in Heinz Zahrnt, *The Question of God*, p. 182.

5 Patriarch

For our last impressions of Barth it is necessary first to return to the Germany of 1946, to a strangely moving scene. It is seven o'clock in the morning of a summer day in the ruins of the once beautiful Kurfürsten Schloss in Bonn, where the university has recently been re-established. The workmen engaged in reconstruction work have not yet settled in for the day. The sound of a hymn breaks the early stillness; a group of solemn-faced students settle back in their chairs. The lecturer, for the first time in his life without a manuscript before him, begins to speak, an elderly man now embarking on his fiftieth semester. The war is over, and Karl Barth has returned to his old haunts to teach once again.[1]

His subject, for the third time in his life, was the Apostles' Creed, and the way in which he approached it was that he had adopted for his *Church Dogmatics* – indeed, the lecture course was later published under the title *Dogmatics in Outline*. The conditions were primitive, but when the course was over, Barth declared that he had never enjoyed himself more.

Was he to stay? After all, until the rise of Hitler all his university experience had been in Germany, and much needed to be done for the reinstatement of theology there. Barth weighed the question, and then made up his mind:

The problem of German reconstruction struck me personally as so vast and as rendered so complicated both by the world around and

87

by the Germans themselves, that I saw myself confronted by an alternative; either to return to Germany for good and devote what time and strength remain to me completely and exclusively to the German problem and the German task; or after all to go at my real work again – namely the continuation and possibly the completion of my *Church Dogmatics* – and to confine my direct participation in German affairs, as well as in other foreign affairs that would inevitably arise, to specific occasions.[2]

The *Church Dogmatics* won.

From now on appears in Barth's occasional writings the note that was struck in a remark of his quoted on the first pages of this book. The *Church Dogmatics* must have priority, and as increasing old age makes a variety of activities impossible, other things will have to go. Whether he is writing a few reminiscences to the Americans or a letter to East Germany, the same thought appears again and again.

What are these *Church Dogmatics*? What do those thirteen large volumes contain?

To attempt to summarize six million words in part of a chapter would be ludicrous. Besides, it would be misleading and unnecessarily discouraging. Barth's own writings, as should be obvious by now, are always better as he wrote them than in the hands of summarizers and interpreters. There is no substitute for reading him directly. The *Dogmatics* is large, but it has already generated its own tourist industry with guides to point out the chief beauty-spots and with package tours for those without the stamina or the independence to make their own exploration.[3] The important thing is actually to set out. What seems much more in place here is to look over Barth's shoulders as he works, so to speak, by making use of the prefaces to individual volumes in which he regularly commented on his aims and his progress.

That means going back even further, for a moment, to 1932, when the first half-volume appeared. Having announced his change of plan, Barth warns his readers that the new approach is to be much more extensive because he wants to give space to indicate the biblical and theological presuppositions of his theology, its place in the history of Christian thought, and the way in which it differs from alternative approaches. All this is to be put in sub-paragraphs in small print, vast jungles of material which have proved a happy hunting ground containing all kinds of unexpected treasures. Passages from the Bible, the fathers and later theologians are quoted in full so that readers can hear directly 'the very voices which rang in my ears as I wrought at my work, which guided, taught and stimulated me, and by which I wish to be measured'.[4]

The work is now called *Church Dogmatics* because Barth wants to demonstrate that dogmatics is not a 'free' science, but one bound to the sphere of the church, where and where alone it is possible and sensible. At the same time, he has cut out everything that might seem to give theology a basis, support or even justification in philosophy (specifically the existentialism which was still a mark of his previous volume). The work is to be conceived on its own, not as part of a school. Here too it seeks to be 'Church'. 'The communion in and for which I have written this book is the communion of the Church, not a theological community of work.'[5]

Barth finally proceeds to outline the course which he expects his project to take, 'If God will and we are alive.' It will be a systematic account of all the areas of Christian doctrine following the method prefigured in *Anselm*. The first volume, 'The Doctrine of the Word of God', of which the first half is now being published, deals with the nature of dogmatics, the use of the word of God as a criterion, with revelation, scripture and the proclamation of the church. Volume II will be 'The Doctrine of God', volume III

'The Doctrine of Creation', volume IV 'The Doctrine of Reconciliation' and volume V 'The Doctrine of Redemption'. I 2 (this is the usual way of referring to volumes and part-volumes) appeared in 1938 and II 1 in 1940; the next preface appears with II 2, written in 1942, ten years after the project began. Barth comments wryly that some of the proofs were corrected by night in a Federal guard-room.[6] One of his fellow-soldiers asked him whether he had brought his carnival paper! Already he has to excuse the size of the book, about which there have been some complaints. He recalls Schleiermacher, struggling over his *Christian Faith*: 'Every time I see this book, I sigh at its bulk,' and consoles himself with Schleiermacher's friend's reply: 'Do not worry; for most of us the size is indispensable to understanding, and the few who would perhaps have understood you from a lesser work will certainly accept with gratitude all the elucidations you want to give.' His own concern is that in places he may not have been long enough.[7]

Already at this point he has had to make some alterations to his plans, where he feels that he has not been faithful enough to his fundamental method; if he had to start from the beginning now, he would have worked differently again. (This feeling persists: while the titles of the volumes remain the same as in the original plan, a comparison of the various forecasts in earlier volumes with what happens later shows that Barth's work is far from being a monolith, conceived in one piece and carried out to a strict design; it is much more like a living organism, developing with a considerable degree of freedom.)

As Barth approaches the doctrine of creation in III 1, published in 1945, he feels much less certain. His rejection of natural theology in any form rules out most traditional approaches, and his basic theological principle makes it 'almost compulsory' that he should present the doctrine in form of an exposition of Genesis 1 and 2. The question of the relationship between these chapters and the scientific view of creation is not discussed. Originally Barth thought that this was going to be necessary, but he later saw 'that there can be no scientific problems, objections or aids in relation to what Holy Scripture and the Christian Church understand by the divine work of creation'.[8] The task of dogmatics is to repeat the old saga. 'There is free scope for natural science beyond what theology describes as the work of the Creator.' Theology moves freely where science has its limit. But the limit is hard to define, and Barth himself has found difficulties here; as a result his treatment of the doctrine of man has been held back for revision.[9]

Work in Germany delayed the appearance of this next volume, III 2, until 1948; it took two further part-volumes, published in 1950 and 1951, to complete Barth's whole treatment of 'Creation'. By this time he had virtually acquired the status of patriarch. He comments that he has become 'almost a legendary instead of an unpopular figure, linked with a good deal of talk about Law and Gospel, East and West, Lutheranism and Calvinism, Infant Baptism and Congregationalism, Bismarck and Frederick the Great' (an indication that he was also involved in more esoteric disputes which it has not been possible to describe here).[10] III 3 deals with divine providence, evil and the angelic world:

It is inevitable that many, impelled perhaps by curiosity, will turn first to the section on angels. If only their perusal is full and scrupulous, and they do not break out too quickly into exclamations at the too much or too little which they think they find there, I have no complaints. But if there are any who begin right at the end, namely, with the demons, they should be told that I regard them as lacking in seriousness . . . I love angels, but have no taste for demons, not out of any desire for demythologization but because they are not worth it.[11]

Behind these almost flippant remarks is another interesting characteristic of Barth's theology; despite his experience of evil in the world, he now talks of it only in terms of nothingness, the *nihil*, the kingdom on God's left hand. He has virtually nothing to say about the positive forces of evil in the terms that many of his contemporaries felt compelled to use.

The contents of III 4, on ethics in the context of creation, are left to speak for themselves, and instead Barth turns to look at the readers which his books have found – 'Even doctors read your dogmatics,' wrote a Dutch student – and the competition in the theological field.[12] The name of Rudolf Bultmann begins to take a prominent place which it maintains in IV 1, the beginning of Barth's treatment of 'Reconciliation', which appeared in 1953. This theme is treated more extensively than ever, for even the part-volumes are further divided into halves. As IV 2 (1955) is followed by IV 3.1 (1959), IV 3.2 (1960) and finally the fragment IV 4 (1968), the prefaces grow more and more autumnal as Barth realizes that the final volume will never be reached. 'I foresee that this book, which by human judgment will be my last major publication, will leave me in the theological and ecclesiastical isolation which has been my lot for almost fifty years. I am thus about to make a poor exit with it. So be it! The day will come when justice will be done to me in this matter too.'[13]

In one of the last prefaces, Barth draws attention to the fact that he is now attaching greater importance to the place of man in the framework of his thinking. The change in this direction is usually dated from the lecture he gave in 1956 on 'The Humanity of God'. However, the change, such as it is, can probably be discovered earlier than this, during the 1940s, in volume II of the *Dogmatics*. That Barth does pay more attention to humanity is certain, but at the same time it is quite clear from the way in which he frames the question he is to answer in the lecture, that his basic presuppositions have not changed. The problem, he affirms, is to derive the knowledge of the humanity of God from the knowledge of his deity – never the other way round.[14] Barth describes his new position as little more than a change of emphasis, and a reading of the lecture through bears that out. For he will not discuss the question of the humanity of natural man; only in and through Jesus Christ can we reach true humanity, and that is the humanity *of God*.

Concentration on the *Church Dogmatics* did not mean that Barth played no part at all in important outside events. One of the surprises of the immediately post-war years is to find him occupying a prominent place at the First Assembly of the World Council of Churches held in Amsterdam in 1948. Surprising because hitherto Barth had had very little interest in the ecumenical movement, though he had already written an introductory paper for the 1937 Faith and Order Conference. He had a rooted suspicion of movements as such, but there was a deeper reason also, namely that his view of the church was not of a kind to further ecumenical development: 'Let the church be the church. When it finds itself under the Word, it will find itself in unity.'[15]

Nevertheless, Barth appeared at Amsterdam. As he says, it happened quite simply. He was asked to co-operate in the theological field and provided a paper for the preparatory study volumes for the Assembly entitled 'The Living Congregation of the Living Lord Jesus Christ'. It is a vintage piece of Barth: church order is discussed only in a negative way, as the clearing away of obstacles to the encounter between God and the congregation through the living Lord Jesus Christ. The congregation itself is seen as 'event', brought about by God in the world (it was this view which led Dr Leonard Hodgson, in criticism, to compare the church on earth with the Cheshire cat in *Alice's Adventures in Wonderland*, and not without reason).[16]

He found the co-operation and co-responsibility at the Assembly 'not only interesting but important', and recalled with satisfaction the value of sitting down at the table with representatives of other churches in an attempt to reach understanding. His own remarks, however, make his position seem more modest than it was; with Professor C. H. Dodd he was in fact invited to speak to introduce the main theme of the Assembly, 'Man's Disorder and God's Design', in the impressive Concertgebouw hall. The official report gives some idea of the scene, before the thousands of delegates representing one hundred and fifty-one churches from forty-two countries and in the presence of Princess Juliana and Prince Bernhard, and also indicates the impression that Barth made in public at the time:

> Prof. Barth spoke in German, often raising his voice and shaking a prophetic finger of warning as he pointed out the danger of all our councils coming to naught unless we kept first things first: first God's Design, which is His and not ours, and must never be confused with any sort of 'Christian Marshall Plan' that we may concoct. 'Should we not come to the clear understanding,' he asked, 'that by "God's Design" is really meant His plan; that is, His already-present, victorious, already-founded Kingdom in all its majesty – our Lord Jesus Christ, Who has already robbed sin and death, the devil and hell of their power, and already vindicated Divine and human justice in His own person? I do not wish to weaken the earnestness, the good will and the hopes that have brought us here, but only to base them on their proper foundation, when I now say: we ought to give up, even on this first day of our deliberations, every thought that the care of the Church, the care of the world, is our care. Burdened with this thought, we should straighten out nothing, we should only increase disorder in Church and world still more. For just this is the final root and ground of all human disorder; the dreadful, godless, ridiculous opinion that man is the Atlas who is destined to bear the dome of heaven on his shoulders.'[17]

Barth went on to say, in a passage not recorded in the Report, that the material presented to the Assembly gave him the impression of being garments of deep mourning. We were not there to mourn. We were there to point to God's kingdom. 'We must be God's witnesses. He has not called us to be his barristers, engineers, managers, statisticians and directors.'[18]

Barth was impatient with the style of the meeting and particularly felt the difference between Anglo-Saxon and Continental ways of thinking. His contributions to discussion were regularly controversial. This controversy continued after the Assembly and was carried on particularly vigorously by Reinhold Niebuhr, who once again voiced a criticism of Barth's neglect of man, and above all man's religious feelings. Barth's theology, he protested, was encapsulated and cut off from the real world. 'We are men and not God', was his slogan, in an attack directed not only against Barth's Amsterdam contributions, but against the whole character of his political thought, as we discussed it in the previous chapter.[19]

Another unexpected journey was Barth's visit to Rome in 1966. He had always been interested in Roman Catholic theology, having made a thorough study of Aquinas as early as his Göttingen days. His (mis)understanding of the Roman Catholic doctrine of analogy, which seemed to him to suggest that God and man by nature shared the same being, led him to maintain a highly critical attitude to many areas of Roman Catholic thought all his days, and this supposed idea of the 'analogy of being' was one which he used to demonstrate when the limits of true theology had been reached; on the other hand, he took constant delight in the growing interest in his work shown by Roman Catholic theologians. He confessed with wonder that 'What-

95

ever a man may think about me otherwise, he will have to grant me the strange fame entailed in the fact that since the Reformation no figure in Protestant theology has aroused so much critical but also positive and in any case serious interest on the part of Roman Catholic scholars.'[20] It was the Roman Catholics, he believed, who had made the most profound evaluations of his work, even when their conclusions differed from his own. Perhaps his greatest surprise was when the young Hans Küng, now one of the leading contemporary Roman Catholic theologians, wrote a study arguing that there was no essential difference between justification by grace as taught by Karl Barth and the doctrine of the Roman Catholic Church, rightly understood. And there had been no official repudiation of this book. What was one to say? Had the millennium broken in? As with many of the studies of his work, Barth consented to write a preface to the book. He could not resist making a characteristic sally at the author. 'Well done,' he remarked, 'but did you come to your conclusions about Roman Catholic doctrine before you read Karl Barth, or after?'[21]

A great honour came when he was asked informally by the Secretariat for Christian Unity in Rome whether he would like to attend the last two sessions of the Second Vatican Council personally, as an observer. Unfortunately, the invitation reached him when he was in hospital, and he was unable to accept. However, the thought of Rome still lingered in his mind, and almost three years later, in May 1966, he decided to supplement his reading of Roman Catholic writers and documents about the Council with some direct information. He therefore wrote and invited himself to Rome for a week's stay, an invitation which was acceded to with alacrity.[22]

As ever, Barth did some careful homework. He studied the sixteen Latin texts produced by the Council and some of the commentaries on them, and then drew up ten series of questions on what he understood the Council to be saying. Armed with these, he set out. Some of the most distinguished Catholic theologians made themselves available for conversations, and with them Barth held a series of seminars. He would present his questions, in written form, and elaborate on them when necessary; then the various Catholic theologians would give their answers, in sessions which often took two or three hours. Barth describes vividly one of the meetings, with the Jesuits, high up in the Gregorian Institute, watching from his chair the rays of the autumn sun picking out the cupola of St Peter's, so that as he talked he could never forget precisely where he was.

Of course, he had a conversation with the Pope himself, at which Barth did not hesitate to produce some more questions, about Roman Catholic teaching on the Virgin Mary and about a phrase that appears frequently in the Council documents, 'separated brethren'. Would the Pope agree with what Barth himself had learnt in Rome, that the word 'brethren' ought to be underlined? The Pope would. The Pope presented Barth with a facsimile copy of the famous Codex Vaticanus text of the gospels; Barth in turn presented the Pope with four of his smaller works. The Pope accepted them with a smile. 'I suppose,' he remarked, 'that it would have been rather laborious for you to have brought along all the *Church Dogmatics*!'

Barth's final words on his Italian visit are worth quoting,

I met *ultra montes* so many Christian people with whom I could not only talk seriously but also have a good laugh that I cannot think without sadness about some of the garden dwarfs on our own pastures. Optimism for the future is not to be entertained. But a quiet, brotherly hope is steadily growing, coupled with a readiness in the meanwhile to wipe our own doorsteps clean in things great and small. There is no sense in 'conversions' to and from the Roman Catholic Church (there are sins within the walls as well as outside them). They only make sense where they take the necessary form of conversions, not to another church, but to Jesus Christ, the Lord of the one, holy, catholic and apostolic church.[23]

By that time, Barth had retired from university teaching. For his last semester, the winter of 1961–62, he departed from his usual practice of delivering as lectures the next forthcoming part of his *Church Dogmatics* and instead wrote, as a swan song, a completely new set of introductory lectures to theology, subsequently published under the title *Evangelical Theology*. They are certainly Barth's most moving book, one of those great 'Indian summer' works that gifted men seem to manage to produce in old age, and an excellent introduction to his thought. Some of the lectures were also delivered, in English, later in 1962, in America. Barth had at last been prevailed upon, at the age of seventy-six, to cross the Atlantic. His son Markus was now teaching theology at the University of Chicago, which provided some incentive, but doubtless Barth's curiosity finally got the better of him.

He lectured at length at Chicago and Princeton, and also gave single lectures in San Anselmo, California, and Richmond, Virginia, combining this with a good deal of sightseeing. At Richmond his detailed knowledge of the battles of the Civil War came as a great surprise to his hosts, who still relate in dumbfounded amazement how he would correct his guides to the battlefields in their accounts of tactics and be proved subsequently to be quite right. Participant, too, he even shouldered a Confederate musket and hit a handkerchief at the range of one hundred feet with it.[24]

One final activity of this incredible man remains to be related. He had ceased to be a parish minister in 1921, and for much of his life showed a notable lack of concern for practical questions of church life, for all his protests to the contrary. Nevertheless, he was not one of those professors

98

of theology who never enter a church. On the contrary, of the two activities to which he gave special priority as long as his health allowed, one was a regular meeting with students, the other was occasional preaching to the prisoners in Basel gaol.

It began in 1954, when Barth accepted an invitation to preach from the prison chaplain, and his visits extended for a period of over ten years. Some thirty of his sermons, most of them delivered at the times of the great festivals, have been collected and published in two volumes, *Deliverance to the Captives* and *Call for God*. They are a far cry from the sermons that were delivered from the pulpit at Safenwil, though their basis is still the same. They are serene, assured, at times even slightly wistful. The world of books is left behind. 'Some of you', Barth tells his congregation, 'have perhaps heard it said that in the last forty years I have written a great many books and that some of them are very fat ones. Let me, however, frankly and openly and even gladly confess that the four words, "My grace is enough", say much more and say it better than the whole pile of paper with which I have surrounded myself. When my books have long since been superseded and forgotten, then these words will still shine on in all their eternal richness.'[25]

In these sermons there is the same immaculate structure that marks all Barth's writing; there is, as on the larger scale of the *Dogmatics*, the consideration of the subject from a variety of perspectives; and there is a clarity and simplicity of language to go with the concentration on what the Bible has to say. For standing above everything is the text itself.

Barth's last sermon in Basel gaol was preached on Easter Day 1964. He chose to speak on the passage in the Gospel of John (20.19f.), in which Jesus appears to the disciples who are shut in behind closed doors. The text ends, 'Then the disciples became glad when they saw the Lord'. Barth comments on this final phrase, first, by referring to his beloved Paul: 'Death, where is your sting? Where, grave, your victory? Thanks be to God who gives us the victory through our Lord Jesus Christ.' Then he goes on:

> They gained a vision of a final breaking of all bonds, of a last and final solution of all riddles, of being recognized and existing in the kingdom of eternal light, whose first ray had touched them and lit their path at that very moment, on that day. For that very reason they became glad when they saw the Lord. That they became glad certainly already meant for them that they might even laugh a little – not at once right over their faces, but continually from then on deep down inside.[26]

It is this gladness, Barth ends, that can come to 'the little Easter congregation of prisoners in Basel's Spitalstrasse with their chaplain and organist, with all the inmates and warders of this institution and (after all, I suppose I belong here too) with the old professor who occasionally pays a visit here'.

One wonders how the congregation received this preaching. Did they really follow the majestic pattern of Barth's sermon? Did they not at times let their attention wander as the words rolled over them; did they not perhaps stretch, shift their position, watch for the signs of the coming conclusion? Did Barth succeed any more in conveying his intended message to them through his words than he had done, fifty years earlier, to the puzzled people of Safenwil? Perhaps not. Probably even Barth's sermons, like so much theology, are creations for the professional, rather than anyone else, to admire. At the same time, however, it is hard to believe that the prisoners of Basel gaol, like the people of Safenwil before them, did not see that they had a great man in their midst, even if they could not see what he saw. If nothing else, the presence of the old professor, his

100

very bearing and attitude, will have conveyed a sense of occasion to those who listened to him. And time and again it may also have been obvious that Barth the man did not stand alone. As one hears his peroration, one is irresistibly caught up to look beyond the present situation, questions suppressed, into another reality, attested in the Bible and down the Christian tradition. Somehow, the beginnings of a vision are unfolded – and is not that what Barth was concerned with all along?

Ill health dogged him to the end of his life, and in his last years he had to resign himself to several stays in hospital. He felt the steady failing of his powers, but while he had strength to write, his humour still shone through, even when he was talking about his illness.

> Somewhere within me there lives a bacillus with the name *proteus mirabilis*, which has an inclination to enter my kidneys, which would then mean my finish. I am certain that this monstrosity does not belong to God's good creation, but rather has first come in as a result of the fall. It has in common with sin and with demons also that it cannot simply be done away with, but can be only just despised, combatted and suppressed. That was and is still the task of the doctors, beside whom also good nurses have worked on me night and day. But the main thing is the knowledge that God makes no mistakes, and that *proteus mirabilis* has no chance against him.[27]

As he accepted the fact that the *Dogmatics* could never be finished, he gently shed the burden of his work.

But not completely. Towards the end of the last year of his life he accepted the invitation of a Roman Catholic professor to lecture during the Week of Prayer for Christian Unity at the Paulusakademie in Zurich, to an audience of Catholic and Reformed theologians. Work on the lecture went on slowly but steadily until the evening of 9 December 1968. That night he wrote in his neat longhand the following words:

101

Israel had its patriarchs: Abraham, who went out in faith from his fatherland and friends to the land that God wanted to show him and indeed did show him. This land promised and given to Israel was, according to the tradition, the land in which the patriarchs lived, sinned, suffered and built altars to the Lord. The church called to repentance must know that God is not the God of the dead, but of the living. 'In him they all live' – from the Apostles to the Fathers of yesterday and the day before. They have not only the right but the relevance to be heard today, not uncritically or in mechanical subjection, but with proper attention.[28]

He began the next sentence, but put down his pen before he had completed it and went to bed. He never woke again. In the early hours of the next morning, 10 December, he died suddenly, but peacefully, in his sleep.

NOTES

1. Karl Barth, *Dogmatics in Outline*, SCM Press 1949, p. 7.

2. *HCM*, p. 56.

3. For a selection, see the books listed in *For Further Reading*.

4. *CD* I 1, p. viii.

5. *CD* I 1, p. xii.

6. *CD* II 2, p. ix.

7. *CD* II 2, p. ix.

8. *CD* III 1, p. ix.

9. *CD* III 1, p. x.

10. *CD* III 3, p. xii.

11. *CD* III 3, p. xi.

12. *CD* III 4, p. xiv.

13. *CD* IV 4, p. xii.

14. *The Humanity of God*, p. 34.

15. *The Universal Church in God's Design*, Amsterdam Study Volume I, SCM Press 1948, p. 72.

16. Leonard Hodgson, *For Faith and Freedom* (one volume ed.), SCM Press 1968, Part Two, p. 118.

17. *The First Assembly of the World Council of Churches*, Official Report, SCM Press 1948, pp. 32f.

18. Karl Barth, 'No Christian Marshall Plan!', *The Christian Century*, 8 December 1948, p. 1333.

19. For an account of Niebuhr's attitude to Barth, see June Bingham, *Courage to Change*, SCM Press 1961, pp. 337ff.

20. *HCM*, p. 69.

21. Karl Barth, Preface to Hans Küng, *Justification*, Burns & Oates 1966.

22. For an account of Barth's visit to Rome, see Karl Barth, *Ad Limina Apostolorum* (in German), EVZ Verlag, Zurich 1967.

23. *Ad Limina Apostolorum*, p. 18.
24. *HCM*, p. 80.
25. Karl Barth, *Call for God*, SCM Press 1967, p. 78.
26. *Call for God*, p. 124.
27. *HCM*, p. 86.
28. Karl Barth, *Letzte Zeugnisse*, EVZ Verlag, Zurich 1969, pp. 70f.

6   Problem

We have now followed Karl Barth's life through to the end and seen some of the characteristics of the man and his thought. Inevitably, some judgments have had to be made in passing on one or other aspect of his work, but there has been no attempt at comprehensive criticism on the way. The reckoning has been left until now. What has Karl Barth contributed to the Christian church of the twentieth century? What is his importance, and for what will he be remembered?

There are those who say that at present there should be no summing up at all. Those who have lovingly seen Barth's *Church Dogmatics* through the press in its English form, his supporters in a largely hostile or indifferent English setting, argue that the time for verdicts has still to come. Barth, they say, is a theologian who cannot be criticized until one has listened to him carefully, grasped his work as a whole and seen the place that it occupies in the whole history of theology. And that is a task that may take decades, indeed centuries, to accomplish.

This view is one that would be near to Barth's own heart. One of his favourite retorts to critical questions was to ask how much of the *Church Dogmatics* his questioner had read, and if the answer was unsatisfactory, he would suggest that a little more reading was in order. To a degree, of course, he was right, and if he was right in the context of German theology, his retort applies all the more in the English situation. For Barth is writing in a different milieu, is asking different questions from those with which most of us are familiar, and therefore needs at least the courtesy of being taken on his own terms.

At the same time, however, it is doubtful whether this means that critical questioning should remain wholly silent or should suffer a moratorium. A number of pressing questions about Barth's work have clearly arisen already, and it is surely perverse to suggest that a man should be excused answering questions simply as a result of the great amount of work he has produced, particularly when that work has been carried on in more than the usual isolation. What if it is all built on inadequate foundations? If that is the case, then the more the bulk, the more unstable it becomes. Anyway, is it not inevitable that some analysis and assessment is going to be made immediately, whether the subject and his trustees welcome it or not? Barth is hardly a writer that one can read for long without forming some definite ideas about his significance and status. To play down the need for and desirability of preliminary assessment is to ignore the facts of opinion making. And if the preliminary assessment shows less than full understanding, that may be preferable to complete misunderstanding in a world where perfection cannot be obtained.

There is a large quantity of published discussions on particular aspects of Barth's writings, but here the obvious course to take is to suggest some criticisms which go to the very heart of the whole theological edifice which Barth has created.

First and foremost comes the question of the isolation in which Barth stands and in which he was aware of standing. The chief characteristic of theology today is its many-sidedness. Unless one concludes that the puzzlement and heart-searching over the nature of Christian belief is a symptom of wholesale disobedience to a clearly expressed divine will or that all other thinkers are unduly complicating matters, one has to expect only part of the truth from any one source. Barth, however, is exclusive and decidedly one-sided. One piece of writing makes the point all too clearly. In 1960, Barth was asked to provide some comments on the future of 'liberal theology', a term which was to exclude existentialist theology, but to cover virtually all the rest of theology apart from that branch which Barth himself represented. What did he regard as being hopeful developments? Who were the writers who seemed to provide a starting-point for further thought? Barth mentioned only four names, and of the four thinkers he named only one was alive when he wrote – and he was a Jew, Martin Buber! The average liberal theologian, Barth remarked, is like a man entering a boat a hundred yards or so above the falls of the Rhine and finding himself drifting past the point of no return. But is this really a fair picture of the contemporary scene? And what does it say of the man who drew it?[1]

Barth's insight into the majesty of God and his emphasis on the Word of God could, and unfortunately did, degenerate into a kind of theological triumphalism. As we have seen, at times he seems to be speaking from so lofty a perspective that all human concerns are ignored. Similarly, his questioning, probing and creative mind, so ready to pick up a theme and express it in a new way, so ready to take a question and formulate it completely differently, led him too often beyond the stage at which discussion was possible. For the ability to reframe a question became the inability to give a straight answer to criticism, the inability to enter into argument, to accept that on some things he might conceivably be mistaken. The inevitable solitude became a deadly isolation.

It seems to be the tragedy of Barth that whereas in his

earlier years he was involved in discussion with numerous colleagues (though even then to a limited degree and usually on ground of his own choosing – as we have seen, he had little patience with those from whom he differed, particularly if they were close to him), as his status grew more and more exalted there was no one to challenge him effectively. As a result, during the period of more than a generation when he and his contemporary Rudolf Bultmann dominated German theology, far too many questions were suppressed which ought to have been taken further, and, having been suppressed, are now emerging with more force than ever. This is a tragedy not only of Barth himself, but of the whole of German theology, which by its paternalistic structure is all too open to the influence exercised by two or three dominant figures.

One would expect the most important contributors to theological progress to shed new light on the future by the possibilities for further exploration which they presented. Now while Barth himself is fully conscious of the need for exploration, the openings that he offers are strictly limited ones.

As we saw Toynbee remark, it is difficult to point to any fruitful positive developments along the line which Barth himself initiated. What has happened among those who might reasonably be labelled 'Barthians' is, rather, a regression. What Barth himself managed to hold together by his own personal stature and genius is apparently incapable of being sustained by his successors. As a result, we have had the phenomenon that Barth's influence has been noticeably negative and his pupils seem as often as not to have been responsible for propagating views which if anything are almost mirror images of what Barth himself taught.

The reasons for this can be seen in the hopes and the teaching methods of Barth himself. Paul van Buren, author of *The Secular Meaning of the Gospel*, an attempt to re-interpret the whole of Christianity in secular terms, made a depressing assessment of Barth's influence. For Barth, he commented, the task of his students was to go on revising the *Church Dogmatics*, re-working them until they were perfect. Those who, like van Buren, could not continue in this direction, had no alternative but to attempt to build an alternative structure on the foundations Barth had left them. And they were inadequate, once the miracle of the God-head's rational communication of himself had been taken away. Virtual atheism was inevitable. 'I sent Barth a precis of *The Secular Meaning of the Gospel*,' van Buren went on, 'and he thought I had betrayed him.'[2]

Barth's teaching, certainly towards the end of his life, heightened the peril. Among his seminars for students, he regularly held one in the English language, for the benefit of those Americans who found the German tongue an obstacle to understanding him. One of his students des-cribed what would happen. The group would meet, at first in Barth's home and later in a room hired from a local restaurant. A student would have prepared a piece of work, a section from one of Barth's own writings of which the student would have made a short precis followed by some questions. After assessing the adequacy of the presentation, Barth would take up the prepared questions for answering, occasionally also allowing questions from others in the group.[3] The formality of the proceedings may seem exces-sive to those used to a more open English or American style of teaching, and it must be remembered that Continental teaching stands in a rather different tradition. Neverthe-less, even when this has been taken into account, it should be clear that the exercise would do nothing to lessen Barth's tendency to monologue.

There are three highlights in Barth's theology: God – whose transcendence he stressed to such a degree; Christ – on whom the whole revelation of God to man is centred; and the Bible – through the medium of which that revelation is communicated. These will, of course, play an important part in any Christian theology, but hardly again, one suspects, as they are found in Barth's work. For his writing about all three shows signs of serious inbuilt weaknesses.

The problem of modern theology is what is technically known as the epistemological question, 'How do we know?', and that question becomes most acute in the form 'How do we know God?' With the rise of modern scientific thinking – not just the natural sciences themselves, but the extension of the scientific approach into the fields of history, sociology, anthropology, psychology and so on – and with the negative conclusions for religious belief reached by nineteenth-century philosophy, the question has become an exceedingly difficult one to answer. Barth was well aware of this from his wide reading in the period. He knew that Kant showed the inadequacy of arguments which claimed that it was possible to have *knowledge* of God, by revolutionizing the concept of knowledge. He knew that Schleiermacher (his lifelong antagonist and *alter ego*) had attempted to demonstrate a way to God through man's religious experience and that the flaw in this approach had been mercilessly shown up by Feuerbach, who explained away man's religious experience as a projection of his own hopes, fears and ideals.

With all these roads blocked off, Barth saw only one possibility left. If man is to have knowledge of God it can only be as a result of the gift of God. In the end, man only knows God because God allows him to. Theology, belief, rest on a miracle.

So far, Barth is surely right. Something of this sort must be said by Christians, if they are to keep constantly in mind

109

what their tradition has struggled to say down the ages, that God is not an object like other objects, a being like other beings, which is in man's grasp. Barth's constant criticism of nineteenth-century theology was justified. It did not see the Godness of God, that God is beyond the utmost that we are able to conceive. Where Barth seems to have gone wrong, however, is in the way he developed his thought from the basic insight into the nature of God, in both positive and negative directions.

Positively, on the miracle of divine revelation, Barth has built a six-million-word edifice of Protestant dogmatics. Dietrich Bonhoeffer, one of the most enthusiastic of his followers, did not live to see more than its beginnings, but even on the basis of that he accused Barth of introducing a positivist doctrine of revelation 'which says, in effect, "Like it or lump it": virgin birth, Trinity, or anything else; each is an equally significant and necessary part of the whole, which must simply be swallowed as a whole or not at all'.[4] Bonhoeffer's criticism is put rather loosely, but one can see what he is driving at. Barth seems to be letting in at the back door what he has driven out at the front; his new edifice is far too like the ones that he has knocked down to make room for it. In some respects it is more treacherous, because the way forward from the miracle of knowledge of God is the dubious 'analogy of faith'. We have seen how problematical that is in Barth's political thought; it is no less so as he turns to think about God himself. There are no obvious building controls for the structure: as one critic has put it, he isolates talk about God not so much to make it incredible as to make it impossible for us to know whether it is incredible or not.[5]

Negatively, Barth has constantly insisted that no knowledge of God is possible at all outside the miracle. Anything that seems to be knowledge of God is knowledge of a false

110

god, an idol. One can see the circumstances which led him to maintain this stand; certainly, it was tactically necessary in Nazi Germany, and it may also be necessary in other situations. But is it always the whole truth? Is alleged knowledge of God outside Jesus Christ really *qualitatively* different in every instance from knowledge of God in Christ as Barth describes it? Cannot man in some circumstances, in some of his aspirations, in some of his experiences, apart from the miracle of grace, come nearer to God than in others? Is there not *something* to be said for the religious, artistic, even humanistic tradition of the world? Does not Barth here become odd man out in the Christian tradition itself? To take the most minor practical point: if knowledge of God is as Barth describes it, how can the Christian talk to his friend and persuade him to share his beliefs and concerns? He cannot point to any hints of God in experience, history, morality, for these are all ruled out of court. All that seems possible is to sit in silence and wait; and if nothing happens, atheism is a perfectly logical conclusion, on Barth's own premises.

What is the alternative?, Barth would retort. How do you get beyond the impasse posed by the nineteenth century? Can you escape the conclusions which nineteenth-century thought force upon you? Surely it is pointless to go back to those battles again? But here Barth would seem to be wrong. Theology in the last decade has found itself forced back to the same problems faced by the nineteenth-century philosophers and theologians, and has found that they do not prove as intractable as Barth imagined. Natural theology will never be what it was two hundred years ago, but in a different form it is certainly on the way back, this time to offer a way out of Barth's own impasse.[6]

The second highlight in Barth's theology is the exclusive importance that he gives to Jesus Christ, the narrow passage

111

in the hour-glass through which all divine communication is challenged. Here criticism can be briefer, and limited to one question. Who is this Jesus Christ of whom Barth so constantly speaks?

Barth himself is almost mystical in the way he talks of Christ. Among his last papers is a 'Testimony to Jesus Christ' which he was asked to write for a French journal in 1968, and in which he set out to explain what Jesus was for him. The three pages that he writes are entirely in metaphorical language. Jesus Christ manifested himself to Christians in the once-for-allness of his existence as the free gift of the covenant bestowed on all men. He bore the sins of the world and of the church in his life and death. He bears the promise of victory. He is the Word of God spoken to all men.[7]

Now these are words which the Christian tradition has used almost from the beginning, so it might seem harsh to single out Barth for not indicating more clearly how they are rooted in experienceable reality. But the Christian tradition before Barth has not laid quite the exclusive emphasis on them that Barth himself demands, nor has it been quite so unconcerned as he about the relationship (or lack of it) between imagery and the Jesus of Nazareth who lived and died in first-century Palestine. As is well known, the 'question of the historical Jesus' has been occupying scholars – and the public – for more than a century and a half, from the beginnings of the story told in Albert Schweitzer's *Quest of the Historical Jesus* to *The Passover Plot* and beyond. Barth, despite this, has been quite disinterested. In 1958 he wrote scornfully of 'the authoritative New Testament men, who to my amazement have armed themselves with swords and staves and once again undertaken the search for the "historical Jesus" – a search in which I now as before prefer not to participate'.[8] Is it truly a viable

112

option to maintain this blissful detachment? Can one of the most crucial questions of modern theology be quietly ignored? Obviously it can, but this happens at the price of great obscurity at the heart of Karl Barth's thought, which neither Barth nor his commentators have yet succeeded in lightening.

Thirdly, we come to Barth's use of the Bible. Here it is easier to come to grips with Barth, because the text of the Bible is tangible and we can see what he sees and read what he reads. Or can we?

Barth made some summary remarks about the Bible in his last lectures, which serve as a starting point:

> The post-biblical theologian may, no doubt, possess a better astronomy, geography, zoology, psychology, physiology and so on than the biblical witnesses possessed; but as for the Word of God, he is not justified in comporting himself in relationship to those witnesses as though he knew more about the Word than they. He is neither president of a seminary, nor the Chairman of the Board of some Christian Institute of Advanced Theological Studies, who might claim some authority over the prophets and apostles. He cannot grant or refuse them a hearing as though they were colleagues on the faculty. Still less is he a high-school teacher authorized to look over their shoulder benevolently or crossly, to correct their notebooks, or to give them good, average or bad marks. Even the smallest, strangest, simplest or obscurest among the biblical witnesses has an incomparable advantage over even the most pious, scholarly, and sagacious latter-day theologian. From his special point of view and in his special fashion, the witness has thought, spoken, and written about the revelatory Word and act in direct confrontation with it. All subsequent theology, as well as the whole of the community that comes after the event, will never find itself in the same immediate confrontation.[9]

These words do no more than sum up a position which Barth had, in essentials, always held. For him the Bible was a *given*; the limits of the canon were ultimate limits to the vehicle of divine revelation, which marked out an area utterly different from the rest of the world. 'What gives the present canon of Holy Scripture its authority?', asked an American student at one of Barth's seminars discussing the first half-volume of the *Church Dogmatics*. 'There is no explanation for authority,' replied Barth; 'The canon is the canon just because it is so.'[10]

This does not mean that Barth is a fundamentalist in his understanding of the Bible, as the next question makes clear. 'What differentiates your understanding of the Word of God from that of a fundamentalist?' Barth replies: 'For me the Word of God is a happening, not a thing. Therefore the Bible must become the Word of God, and it does this through the work of the Spirit.'[11] His understanding of the nature of scripture is a sophisticated one, based on his concept of revelation. Revelation, as we have seen, is God's disclosure of himself in Jesus Christ. But since the death of Jesus, revelation is in the past, and has to be proclaimed by the church. Those who proclaim it are, first, the apostles and prophets, and later, the preachers of the church. There is a cardinal difference between the two. The testimony of the prophets and apostles has been recorded in the Bible; once canonized, this Bible remains the permanent basis for proclamation on which the church may draw. As Barth indicated above, however, revelation and scripture are never essentially linked; even through scripture, revelation happens as an event.

But will Barth's position stand up to the findings of historical criticism? Indeed, does he take any notice of historical criticism at all? From the beginning Barth has paid at least lip service to the work done by scholars over the past century in discovering the circumstances in which the Bible came into being. In the preface to the second edition of *Romans* he even went so far as to say that 'the critical historian needs to be more critical'.[12] In his actual writings, however, it is difficult to find any indication that he has taken his own advice; any indication that he seriously concerned himself with historical criticism again after his

114

student days. A passing remark to Thurneysen in his early days seems to be much nearer the mark: 'How frightfully indifferent I have become about the purely historical questions.'[13] Yet his remarks in the paragraph quoted above are precisely about historical questions and represent an opinion which can or cannot be maintained, depending on the findings of *historical* investigation. Such investigation makes them highly dubious. The Bible, authorities on the Old and New Testaments would say, is a collection of the literature of a tradition beginning in Judaism and ending in Christianity, which was given canonical status as a result of certain historically conditioned decisions and on the basis of the community's practice supported by a variety of (often specious) arguments. Many attempts have been made to explain what it is that gives the canon its unity, but 'direct confrontation with revelation', which is the one that Barth puts forward, just will not do. The documents of the New Testament represent a stage of reflection, human reflection, on an event which is already by then in the past. To say that the Pastoral Epistles, II Peter or Jude have 'an incomparable advantage' over modern theologians is nothing short of arrant nonsense, particularly when at the same time they are put in an essentially different category from the contemporary writings of Ignatius of Antioch and I Clement. Such a remark can only be sustained if the books in question – and a good deal of the rest of the Bible – are interpreted in a most unnatural way.

'Unnatural' is in fact an adjective which comes constantly to mind as one reads Barth's interpretation. Like other theologians who isolate the Bible and then lay enormous stress on its normativeness, he is, when he is not being selective, forced to extreme lengths in dealing with some of its less rewarding passages in an attempt to extract 'the meaning'. Like others who wish to have the Bible only as their guide, he has to get round the fact that 'to outward, human, seeming the Bible, and even the New Testament, does not look like a book which conveys a single coherent body of truth';[14] rather than sift the wheat from the chaff in the text as it stands, his solution is to break away, by means of dialectic and analogy, to a new and 'spiritual' level. One can see his procedures as early as *Romans*, in the preface to the third edition of which he has an argument with Bultmann. Bultmann points out that other voices are to be discerned in Paul's writings than that of Christ: Jewish, Hellenistic, those of the surrounding culture, and that therefore criticism has to be made of the content of what Paul is saying at the literal level. Barth retorts that *all* the words of Romans are 'other voices', yet at the same time, through the spirit, they are the voice of Christ.[15]

Yet again, he breaks loose from the realities of the human situation into that heavenly dimension in which he seems to become so arbitrary and so difficult to grapple with. His lifelong preference for books and ideas rather than people and situations (despite all his protests to the contrary!) apparently make him forget that Christianity (and Judaism before it) did not start from a miraculous revelation from heaven, by-passing all human faculties, and an exalted, special book, but was worked out through human lives and histories and insights in a process which always has been and always will be imperfectly carried on. Is the tragedy of Barth that he is looking for an impossible, unattainable perfection in a world where by its and our very nature we have to be content with approximations? Is it, dare one say, that he spent too long sitting at a desk?

The discussion could be continued. But perhaps enough has now been said to show that in the three major areas that have been singled out for inspection, Barth's theology appears to be badly flawed. These flaws are becoming more obvious as time goes on, and to the theological world at large the name of Karl Barth does not mean what it did even ten years ago. Does that, then, suggest that before too long Karl Barth will be only one more theological name, a distinguished member of the breed but no more memorable than the countless figures from the last two centuries who appear as little more than footnotes to doctoral theses?

It is hard to believe so. It seems probable that those who see the *Dogmatics* as a work that will come into its own in future years are over-optimistic. It is not the kind of book for that. Nor is Barth the prophet likely to have the same impact in the years to come that he had in the 1920s. Both Barth the patriarch and Barth the prophet will pass into history as Barth the problem.

Precisely because he is a problem, however, he will surely still be read, for despite the inadequacies in his solutions, the questions that he continually asks are ones that nag away when less rigorous theologies seem to be making the going too easy. And if the system and the principles on which it is based are rejected, the man himself and the reality that he attempted to describe will still be treasured. Whether the writings are his early lectures, *The Word of God and the Word of Man*, and the commentary on *Romans*, or the later *Dogmatics* and *Evangelical Theology*, people who are concerned about the question of God will go back again and again to savour the beauty and the joy that they will find there. And they will find satisfaction not only because of what they begin to see but also because of the character and stamp of the man with whom and through whom they begin to see it. For just as Barth is not Barth without his overriding theological concern, so his theology is not complete without the man himself, who had a greater part in it than he ever realized.

How would he have turned out had he given more play to the world of man and his achievements? Had he felt able to move in this direction he might have been more true to his own nature and the creative gifts with which he was endowed. We have seen occasional expressions of his delight in the world around him when he was not overburdened with his theology; as a postscript there is one last love to be added, so much a love that it points to a real alternative course that even his theology might have followed.

No one can present a rounded picture of Barth without giving a place of honour to Wolfgang Amadeus Mozart. Mozart's music, as we saw at the beginning of this book, had priority in Barth's full day; the composer himself evoked eulogies of a warmth that falls little short of Barth's descriptions of the glory of the heavenly world. Mozart even finds his way into the *Dogmatics* – no less than five times. In one passage, where he is writing about the problem of evil in terms of 'God and nothingness', Barth reflects on how strange it is that on only a few occasions can we see that the creation is good. At this point he breaks off to rhapsodize on – Mozart:

Why is it that this man is so incomparable? Why is it that for the receptive, he has produced in almost every bar he conceived and composed a type of music for which 'beautiful' is not a fitting epithet: music which for the true Christian is not mere entertainment, enjoyment or edification, but food and drink; music full of comfort and counsel for his needs; music which is never a slave to its technique nor sentimental, but always 'moving', free and liberating because wise, strong and sovereign? Why is it possible to hold that Mozart has a place in theology, especially in the doctrine of creation and also in eschatology, although he was not a father of the Church, does not |seem to have been a particularly active Christian and was a Roman Catholic, apparently leading what might appear to us a rather frivolous existence when not occupied in his work? It is possible to give him this position because he knew something about creation in its total goodness that neither the real fathers of the Church nor our Reformers, neither the orthodox nor Liberals, neither the exponents of natural theology nor those heavily armed with the

'Word of God', and certainly not the Existentialists, nor indeed any other great musicians before and after him, either know or can express or maintain as he did . . . Mozart enables us to hear that creation praises its master and is therefore perfect.[16]

To this passage some Dutch Neo-Calvinists objected, using 'unrepeatable terms in disparagement of W. A. Mozart'. Barth retorted: 'In so doing they have, of course, shown themselves to be men of stupid, cold and stony hearts to whom we need not listen.'[17]

Barth wrote four independent pieces about Mozart.[18] In one of them he relates how he first heard Mozart about the age of six, when his father played on the piano a few bars of 'O my Tamino', from *The Magic Flute*. It was the beginning of a love affair in which there was 'Mozart and no one else'.[19] In 1956, on the two hundredth anniversary of Mozart's death, he was invited several times to write and speak about the composer. In a letter of thanks he wrote, 'You have repeatedly given me, a human being of the twentieth century, courage (not haughtiness!), tempo (not exaggerated tempo!), purity (not boring purity!) and peace (not complacent peace!)'[20] Elsewhere he wondered at the source of Mozart's music. How does he know all that he expresses when he has no interest in nature, history or the other arts, politics, landscape, architecture? He does not want to proclaim the praise of God, but he does just that in being an instrument; he is a parable of the kingdom of heaven.[21] As a final word of praise the scene is shifted to heaven itself: 'Whether the angels play only Bach in praising God I am not quite sure; I am sure, however, that *en famille* they play Mozart, and then also God the Lord is especially delighted to listen to them.'[22]

One cannot make a theology out of Mozart, but who knows what might have happened if Barth had not been compelled by his battles against liberal theology and Nazi

Germany to establish a barrier between the revelation of God and human culture and instead had extended his insights here into other areas of human creativity?

We shall never know. Or perhaps we might. Barth once said that when he reached heaven there were a number of figures whom he wanted to meet: Augustine, Thomas Aquinas, Luther, Calvin, Schleiermacher, but before all of them he would first enquire about Mozart.[23] If there were not too much of a crowd, it would be marvellous there to talk to Barth himself, not about his theology as it is, but as it might have been; to listen to a little Bach and then some Mozart; and then perhaps to see if it were possible to persuade him to extend his repertoire a little wider.

NOTES

1. Karl Barth, 'Liberal Theology: Some Alternatives', *The Hibbert Journal*, 1961, pp. 213–19.

2. In Ved Mehta, *The New Theologian*, p. 111.

3. John D. Godsey, *Karl Barth's Table Talk*, Oliver & Boyd 1963, p. viii.

4. Dietrich Bonhoeffer, *Letters and Papers from Prison*, rev. ed., SCM Press 1967, p. 157.

5. David Jenkins, *Guide to the Debate about God*, Lutterworth Press 1966, p. 81.

6. For further criticism see Heinz Zahrnt, *The Question of God*, pp. 118ff.

7. *Letzte Zeugnisse*, pp. 7–9.   8. *HCM*, p. 69.

9. *Evangelical Theology*, p. 34.   10. *Table Talk*, p. 26.

11. Ibid.   12. *Romans*, p. 8.

13. *RTM*, p. 36.

14. D. E. Nineham, 'The Use of the Bible in Modern Theology', *Bulletin of the John Rylands Library*, 1969, p. 185; the whole article contains some important criticisms of Barth.

15. *Romans*, pp. 16f.   16. *CD* III 3, pp. 297f.

17. *CD* III 4, p. xiii.

18. Collected in Walter Leibrecht (ed.), *Religion and Culture: Essays in Honour of Paul Tillich*, SCM Press 1959, pp. 61–78.

19. *Religion and Culture*, p. 61.   20. *Religion and Culture*, p. 63.

21. *Religion and Culture*, p. 69.   22. *Religion and Culture*, p. 64.

23. *Religion and Culture*, p. 61.

For Further Reading

Books by Barth

The Word of God and the Word of Man, Harper Torchbooks
   1957
The Epistle to the Romans, OUP 1933
Revolutionary Theology in the Making (ed. J. D. Smart),
   Epworth Press 1964
From Rousseau to Ritschl, SCM Press 1959
Dogmatics in Outline, SCM Press 1949
Against the Stream (ed. R. Gregor Smith), SCM Press 1954
Deliverance to the Captives, SCM Press 1961
Evangelical Theology, Fontana Books 1965
How I Changed my Mind, St Andrews Press 1969; and, of
   course, *Church Dogmatics*, T. & T. Clark, 1936–69 (see
   also *Church Dogmatics: A Selection*, ed. H. Gollwitzer,
   T. & T. Clark, 1961)

Books about Barth

T. F. Torrance, *Karl Barth: An Introduction to his Early
   Theology 1910–1931*, SCM Press 1962
A. B. Come, *An Introduction to Barth's Dogmatics for
   Preachers*, SCM Press 1963
H. Hartwell, *An Introduction to the Theology of Karl Barth*,
   Duckworth 1965
H. Zahrnt, *The Question of God*, Collins 1969

Index

123